Getting Personal

Other titles by Kathy Galloway:

Imagining the Gospels (SPCK/Triangle 1987, 1994)
Love Burning Deep (SPCK 1993)
Struggles to Love (SPCK 1994)

Getting Personal

Sermons and Meditations (1986–94)

KATHY GALLOWAY

First published in Great Britain 1995
Society for Promoting Christian Knowledge
Holy Trinity Church
Marylebone Road
London NW1 4DU

ACKNOWLEDGEMENTS

Scriptures quoted from the *Good News Bible* (GNB)
published by The Bible Societies/HarperCollins Publishers Ltd UK
© American Bible Society, 1966, 1971, 1976, 1992.
Quotations from *The Jerusalem Bible* © 1966 by
Darton, Longman & Todd Ltd and Doubleday and Co. Inc.

Lines on page 55 and page 96 by John L. Bell,
Wild Goose Worship Group, the Iona Community.
Used with kind permission.

Lines on page 99 by Kate Compston from
Bread of Tomorrow, ed. Janet Morley (SPCK 1992).

British Library Cataloguing-in-Publication Data
A catalogue record for this book is available from the
British Library

ISBN 0-281-04847-9

Typeset by
Pioneer Associates Perthshire, Scotland
Printed in Great Britain by
The Cromwell Press Melksham, Wiltshire

getting personal,
for Val

Contents

Preface

These writings – sermons, editorials from *Coracle,* the magazine of the Iona Community which I have edited for the last five years, imaginative dialogues, and one long article – have all been written in the context of ongoing relationships. The sermons were mostly preached, either in Iona Abbey during the time I was Warden there and subsequently as a visiting member of the Community, or in Lansdowne Parish Church in Glasgow, the local Church of Scotland where I am a member. I wish to thank successive Wardens of the Abbey and the MacLeod Centre on Iona for inviting me to preach, and the people of Landsdowne Church who have been for me, as for many others, a source of acceptance, encouragement and down-to-earth constancy as I rush around the country getting off trains from time to time. Visiting local churches and groups in many places, and enjoying meetings which are warm, renewing and frequently inspiring but of necessity passing moments, it matters a lot to belong to a community of faith to go from and to return to.

The same is true of belonging to the more extended network of the Iona Community. As a member for many years, I know that I am always challenged, sustained and changed by its web of connection, and by the numerous people who weave that web across Britain and beyond. All my writing, not just in *Coracle,* indeed all my living, has as its seedbed the incarnational theology, the commitment to healing the splits between the personal and the political and the desire to find new ways to touch the hearts of all, which its members seek to give flesh to in their own lives, and which has been given such notable expression in the writing of George MacLeod and Ralph Morton. I thank them both, and all the members of the Community, for helping me to find a living language for my faith.

I wish to thank the staff at SPCK, and especially Philip Law, who has been helpful and encouraging in the best editorial fashion.

Most of all, I wish to thank my father, Jack Orr. In thirty years of parish ministry in a new housing scheme in Edinburgh, he never wrote a book, never became renowned as a preacher (though he is a good one), or indeed, theorized very much at all. But he did encourage hundreds of men and women *and* children, including me, to believe that they had things worth expressing and being listened to about their faith and their lives, and, in the conviction that liturgy is the work of the people, trusted them and enabled them to preach, pray, teach, sing and speak. And they were worthy of that trust. In a largely working-class parish, I learned far more about worship and preaching from the experience of seeing many people doing it than I ever did in theological college or from books. That, in the end, seems to me a more significant achievement than even the best sermon.

This collection is entitled 'Getting Personal', from the title of one of the sermons. But it is more than a name. It is a personal conviction, a way of life. I like getting personal. It is, for me, what makes life most worth living. It's what I like best about Jesus, that he was always getting personal. Sometimes, getting personal is a little frowned upon, a little suspect, a little what women are supposed to do. I have never, for the life of me, been able to see the advantages of impersonality (which is not necessarily the same as objectivity), especially in a world which is so terribly alienating and divided. We all speak and act from our own experience, our own context. Better by far to acknowledge that frankly, and to look for the extension and increase of our knowledge and experience and for listening to that of others, than to claim an impartiality we cannot in reality own. Nor have I found that getting personal reduces or negates the need for corporateness. I have found that the reverse is true, that the more personal we are, the more we have to confront the needs and claims of the community. We are persons in community, and we are most known in personhood in relationship. To love a person is also to be concerned about the community in which he or she must live. To neglect one is to neglect the other. The personal is always political – but the political only becomes real, not theoretical, when it is grounded in the personal.

I think this is also true of the love of God.

PART ONE

Getting Personal

1
Getting Personal

Jeremiah 29.1, 4–14; Philippians 3.7–21; John 17.1–10

What interesting readings this morning, about three pretty desperate situations. First, a man writing to a whole people taken prisoner, driven into exile, forced labour for a foreign invading power. Second, a man in prison, a prisoner of conscience you might say, writing to the small, struggling community he had established from far away, knowing that they were split by internal factions, and wandering far from their original vision. Third, a man having a last meal with his friends, knowing that he had been betrayed by one of them, and was facing imminent arrest and possible death at the hands of a hostile establishment.

Three situations of extremity, none of them at all unfamiliar to the world of 1993. But these three situations are far apart in time, removed from our time and removed from each other. The first man was Jeremiah, writing to the priests, civil servants and skilled workers of the people of Israel, basically, all the leadership, who had been driven off into exile in Babylonia by King Nebuchadnezzar. Jeremiah, the reluctant prophet, was writing them instructions from the Lord as to how they were to cope with their captivity. The second man was Paul, writing to the church at Philippi, encouraging, exhorting, also giving them instructions, using his own experience to inspire them to greater faith. And the third man, Jesus, in the upper room after sharing the Passover meal? Well, Jesus was praying for his friends. Jesus was always very personal. It's one of the most attractive things about him.

Three responses to desperate situations, and they may well strike chords with you, as they do with me. Words of hope for

3

exile. Words of encouragement from prison. Words for friends in the face of death. Let's listen to these words a little more carefully, and see whether they are words for us also.

First of all Jeremiah, giving pretty sensible, practical advice. First, he suggests that there is learning to be done in this apparently hopeless situation, perhaps even a bit of *realpolitik* – you, the people of Israel, brought this catastrophe upon yourselves by your greed and injustice, now you have to deal with the consequences, because the Lord's not going to sweep down and rescue you. So you better just get on with your lives in exile, build houses, settle down, marry, have lots of children, work for the cities you find yourselves in, because if they do well, you'll do well. And ignore the false prophets who tell you they can predict the future. The future is in the hands of God. And then, when the time is right, and only God knows when that will be, you will come home. And because you *are* in exile, because the sense of not being in the right place, the desire for at-home-ness still aches deep within you, you will look for the Lord, and the Lord will find you and call you home.

Hard words, these, unyielding even, and yet words of hope too. I think that Jeremiah, listening for the word of the Lord that burned deep within him in a time of social and political upheaval was saying something like, '. . . live your exile, learn from it, don't waste it in trying to predict or hurry or impose the future, and trust God to bring you home at the right time, when you have discovered what it really means to seek God.'

Perhaps they are still useful words for people in exile, whether it is exile from a geographical land, or the land of employment, or the land of social acceptance or from right relationship, or whatever exclusion is experienced as exile. Live in the present, not the past or the future, but don't deny the ache of exile either, because it's part of what will lead you home with and to God.

And then there's Paul, in prison, under constraint, with little apparent freedom. And yet there he is, not talking about his losses, but about his gains, about being a citizen of heaven, and not sounding at all like a captive. Less a captive, in fact, than those who have liberty in external things but no liberation in their drivenness and addictions. He gives advice too, drawn from his experience and his listening for the voice of the Holy Spirit. Paul's advice is curiously like Jeremiah's in some respects. He too says, don't get stuck in the past, keep going, run the race, live your life, go forward, concentrate on how you run, follow the wisdom you already have. I sometimes imagine that for Paul, as for a lot of brave and committed people in prison, it was very important to have little communities of people on the outside who looked to him, cared about him, needed him. Because, with the best will in the world, there must have been many moments of frustration, fear, disappointment, even moments when he felt like giving up. But his connectedness with these little communities of faith, struggling, suffering, quarrelling, needing constant encouragement, perhaps enabled him to dig even deeper into his resources of faith and hope, draw upon his love for them, and draw him out of his own immediate predicament. Their need brought out the best in him, and in responding to them, perhaps he himself was renewed in faith and hope.

Useful words, Paul's, for people imprisoned, perhaps by iron bars, or perhaps by the iron bars of illness, lack of opportunity or whatever kinds of constraints are experienced as lack of freedom. Find in the connectedness with those who struggle and suffer, nearby or far away, a love which has the power to go beyond the self and so can release the self.

And Jesus? I find it hugely reassuring that Jesus was so personal. It is our most human response in times of acute crisis or danger, to think about those we love, are closest to – and here is Jesus, putting in a good word for his mates in the most impassioned tones. Remember all the obtuseness of the disciples, their failure to understand him, their confusion. Remember their chequered histories, the dubious backgrounds of some of them. Remember the times he got angry with them, told them off, despaired of them. Well, here he is now, saying to God, they have been attentive to him, they have received, they have believed. All the disagreements, all the frailties, that's not important now. What matters is the relationship that has been forged in three years of walking the way, of tramping the dusty roads of Palestine, not always knowing where the next meal was coming from; three years of miracle and mockery, of laughter and tears, of fear and freedom, of danger and delight. Three years of companionship, of intimacy, of friendship, of learning, of struggle. Of course you would grow to love these people who had shared your life. Of course you would get personal.

All over the world, today, at this moment, there are people praying for those they love, there are people getting personal. People praying for their dying children, for their lost parents, for their lovers in danger, for their friends who are sick or hungry or diseased or tormented or tortured. All over Africa, people on a knife-edge are getting personal. Getting personal *can* mean wrapping our loves, our friendships round us like a security blanket to keep out the cold winds blowing, can mean building a wall of protection to huddle behind. Or it can mean, as it did for Jesus, setting up a chain reaction of love, igniting out into all the world a warmth to help us confront the cold winds, an encouragement to go beyond the walls of protection. The choice is ours. We can put ourselves in the picture of the Bible stories, and believe that they include us. We can put ourselves in the picture of this weary, hungry aching world that is desperately longing to get more personal, to stop being about numbers and statistics and types and problems and causes and be *real*, and believe that the picture includes us. Or we can blank ourselves out of the stories of people in exile or in prison or facing death, blank ourselves out of the pictures of Africa and Bosnia and the homeless people on Great Western Road. We can simply disconnect. The choice is ours. But if we disconnect from other people, we disconnect from God, and *we* become the prisoners with no release, the exiles always living in the past and the future but never today, the ones who are only waiting for death and who are not connected with the fullness of life.

Jeremiah and Paul and Jesus all cared about the way we live *now*, and were content to trust God about the outcome. They all spoke about prayer, and the importance of the yearning for connection with God which moves us to pray. They all lived connected by bright threads of love with communities great or small, nearby or far away. Today, *we* are invited to get personal, to think about how we live now and how that affects other people; to pray for insight into *how* to love now; to think about how we respond to the aching needs of persons in communities in Africa and other far away places, because of, and as an extension of, the love we have known personally. God guide us all. Amen.

Lansdowne Church, Glasgow, 20th Sunday after Pentecost, 1993.

2
Freddy's Story

Once upon a time there was a boy called Freddy who was very shy. The reason he was so shy was that he thought he was ugly – so ugly, in fact, that no one would ever love him. Freddy decided that in order to stop people laughing at him (which he thought they were bound to do, him being so ugly and all) he would disguise himself with so many clothes that nobody would recognize him.

First, he put on a great big hairy jumper, then he put on a great big heavy overcoat that went right down to his ankles. He looked at himself in the mirror, but he was still worried that he might be recognized; so he found a hat that came right down over his forehead, and a pair of dark glasses to hide his eyes. Finally, just so that any impertinent strangers would definitely get the message, he invested in a huge radio, and played it at full volume whenever anyone came near him. By this time, it goes without saying, Freddy was extremely hot and sticky, and in a thoroughly bad temper, so his red and furious gaze was enough to deter almost anyone. He slouched around, carrying his huge radio, and everyone left him well alone. As you can imagine, he now looked so peculiar that he had achieved that which he most wished to avoid – drawing attention to himself. But nobody came near him, they just stared. And Freddy, behind his dark glasses, felt that he had indeed made himself invisible.

Then one day, when he was sitting in the park disturbing the peace, a girl walked past him on her way home. As she passed the curious figure, she turned and looked at him, and she caught him looking at her from between his hat and his glasses. Her attention was held, and the next day, when she came that way again, she looked for him. Freddy, in the meantime, who in spite of his disguise was really horribly lonely, had fallen in love with her at first sight, and his little heart was pounding away under all the layers. However, old habits die hard, and when he saw her approaching he panicked, and turned his radio up. The girl stopped beside him and started to speak, but of course he could hear nothing. She began to shout, and finally, in exasperation, she pulled the earphones out of his ears. Piteously he tried to hang on to them, but she took them firmly out of his grasp and put them down. Then she sat beside him on the bench and began to talk.

Going home that night, Freddy was so excited that he gave his radio to a passing tramp. And he heard the birds singing for the first time in ages.

The next day, they met again in the park, and the day after, and then one day the girl (who was called Sally) asked him to take his glasses off so that she could see what colour his eyes were. Fearful that she would see how ugly he was, he took them off, but all she said was how blue his eyes were. He left the glasses decorating a statue in the park, and he noticed as they walked back together that night that she had a scar on her cheek, and he felt sorry that somehow she had been hurt at some time.

The next weekend they went for another walk, and it started to rain, so he gave her his hat to stop her getting wet and catching a cold. Sally told him that she loved dancing, and suggested that they might go to a place she knew where they played great dance music. Freddy was shocked to the core at the idea of making a spectacle of himself in that way. But he went anyway, and realized as they were going in that if he tried dancing in his overcoat he might well expire from the heat. They had a little argument at the door, but he wanted Sally to have a good time, and so he hung up his coat in the cloakroom, and got so engrossed in learning how to dance that he forgot all about it when they left, and went home without it.

As they walked home together, they talked about all kinds of things, and when they got to the door, she told him that she wanted to hug him, but that she wasn't going to let herself be scratched by his horrible hairy jumper, and would he please take it off. Freddy had worn it for so long that it really hurt him to take it off, and he stood there for a few minutes feeling as if he had nothing on (although, of course, he did) but then she put her arms round him, and he thought about how much less enjoyable this would be if he still had his big scratchy jumper on, and then he quite forgot about it altogether.

Freddy didn't quite have the nerve to throw his jumper away, and from time to time, when he was feeling low, or feeling sorry for himself, he would put it on again, but then he always found himself remembering what it was like to hug someone without it. And he would take it off, and go out and find someone to hug – not always Sally, but someone, because by now he had discovered that there were quite a lot of people around who were keen on hugging, *even* on hugging him. And he spent a lot of time trying to persuade people that hugging without scratchy jumpers was an experience never to be missed. And, mostly, they found that they agreed with him!

Iona Abbey, 1987.

3
Jesus Was Young

Do not let anyone look down on you because you are young,
but be an example for the believers in your speech, your
conduct, your love, faith and purity. (1 Timothy 4.12, GNB)

Jesus was young. That fact always strikes me with some force
whenever I remember it. At least, young by Western standards,
though judged by Ethiopia or Bangladesh you might say he was
getting on towards middle age. But in Britain, he would be too
young to be the Prime Minister, or even the leader of a party, too
young to be a general or a bank manager or the chairman of the
board, and eyebrows would certainly be raised, and are, when
someone of his age is appointed the president of a trade union or
the headmaster of a school. Our society would consider him too
young for real power.

And not only was he young, he didn't even show any of the
marks of the rising young man, any of the signs that might have
endeared him to his elders. He was unemployed, and, what was
worse, he had voluntarily given up a perfectly good trade to go
wandering round the countryside with no fixed address – a kind
of early New Age traveller. He had no home, having left his
family with some rather ungrateful and not at all 'family values'
comments about anyone who did God's will being his family. He
was not married, had no children, and was a perfect target for
accusations of irresponsibility and refusing to play his part in the
upholding of society.

His friends were questionable, and in some cases downright
disreputable, including as they did criminals, drunks and prostitutes. He spoke out strongly against the status quo, the establishment, and corruption in high places – in the government, in the
military, in the church. He refused to take part in a military upris-
ing, and would not defend himself when attacked. He spoke a

great deal more about money than he did about sex. He did all
the things that we warn our children against doing, and very
much about him went completely against the standards of success and status we set for young people. And not only did he do
these things himself, he also actively encouraged other people to
do them too. He invited people to go and give away all their
money to the poor and join him in his vagabond life. He told
them to leave their jobs and their families and their security and
opt for a life of uncertainty. If we met him today, we might be
warned against him as a bad influence on young people, and
there would probably be a police file on him.

He had qualities which we tend to ascribe to youth (often in
order to dismiss them) – idealism, a quick temper, a tendency to
do things on the spur of the moment (have you ever noticed how
often Mark's Gospel describes Jesus as doing something 'imme-
diately', and how often he changes his plans, when he had any,
that is?). What an irritant, how infuriating he must have been to
the power-holders and power-brokers, this young upstart from an
unfashionable place.

The church, most of the time, has tried to pretend that Jesus
wasn't young. Sometimes, it has just ignored the fact, and has
acted as if Jesus was a grave, sober, impressive elderly man.
Many Protestants like this notion of Jesus. Elderly men in black
suits preside over what bears more relationship to a funeral than
a celebration, and dignity is the most important thing. We are
exhorted in suitably elderly, even archaic language, to adhere to
ways of doing things that have happened for generations, without
the question ever being asked if this way of doing things is
actually speaking to the real needs of people.

Or sometimes, the church has acknowledged that Jesus was
young, but has still managed not to let it make a difference, by
saying, in effect, well, yes, true, he *was* young, but he was different, so it doesn't count. As if it were accidental, a little mistake
on God's part. But isn't the incarnation, the life of Jesus, about
the fact that Jesus was born like us? So, if he was young, not an
old man in disguise or some kind of freak young man, then he
really was a young man, with all that that implies. Is it not the
case that what was different about Jesus was not the nature of his
humanity, but the choices he made about its expression? Young
man as he was, all the humanity and youthful quality of his life
was offered up to witness to a radically different understanding

of the world from that in which he stood. By being who he was, not in spite of who he was, he did what he did. The unique quality of a young man's love offered other possibilities for justice, for transformation, for a new way of being human. Freely choosing not to act out of his own urges for self-fulfilment, not enslaved to the gratification of his own desires, but equally not bound to any political or social system, any religious orthodoxy, not imprisoned in any dogma or doctrine, he chose a way that led to pain, humiliation, dreariness and death. Not because any of these things were good or desirable, because none of them are, but because they were the consequence and cost of that way. I find demonstrated in that way, at one and the same time, both a sacrificial commitment to the value and worth of people, and indeed of all that is created, which we might choose to call unconditional love, *and* a profound assertion of his own calling, worth, freedom, self. At the moment of most complete self-surrender, he was most completely himself.

Did he struggle with these choices? Every step of the way. Did he find them easy, pleasant, inevitable? Not according to the Gospels. He fought with God and angels and demons, as well as with great social and political forces. He dissented, groaned, sweated, shouted and despaired. No wonder he needed times of deep solitude – and no wonder that he liked parties and feasts so much, when he could simply relax and let things just be.

But through all the tension and conflict, he returned again and again to that freedom and that demand which would not let him go. And from the abandonment of all ambition for his own happiness, success and power came the new life of resurrection, in which all that is surrendered is given back in new, mysterious, but real ways.

The very fact of Jesus' age makes this self-surrender all the more an act of love. It is hard to let go of life at any age. But voluntarily to give up all the possibilities that youth offers, to choose not to drink the cup of living to the full – there is a choice few of us would make willingly. Too many have that decision forced on them. It is not twenty-year-olds who decide to make wars, but they are most often the ones sent to fight and die. There is nothing good or noble about the curtailment of life by war, hunger, injustice, cruelty. And for Jesus, aware of the power he had, and could have to a much greater extent, feeling perhaps that there was so much good he could still have done, the pain of surrender must have been acute. Renunciation, for anyone, and for the young man Jesus too, is never easy. Only love and the exercise of freedom gives it any meaning.

I stress Jesus' youth not to slight or offend older people. For the rest of my life, I will be older than Jesus. And his good news, and the invitation to be part of the community of faith, was to people of all ages. But it is important that we allow ourselves to be challenged by the person of Jesus, in a world where being young is often seen as being a barrier to real responsibility, and where we think we can lay down what our young people should be like from a desire to relive our own youth.

And so, when we read the Gospels, we need to look at our own communities and cities and ask, where is the young Jesus to be found? Is it in the seats of power and authority? Or could it be that we see him, as in the Gospels, questioning the status quo, offending the respectable, outraging and threatening the mighty with his revolutionary message of love and justice and forgiveness, with his continual call to change economic priorities away from favouring the rich towards justice for the poor? And where do we find Jesus' contemporaries in the church? Are they pushed to the margins, denied a voice, unheard in the name of one who was too young to be a bishop or a church dignitary? Are our churches places where both young and old can meet a young Jesus, and not simply his pale ghost? If we are honest, we know that most of Jesus' contemporaries never come near the church. They are to be found elsewhere. Instead of lambasting them for whatever imagined failing this denotes, we might more usefully consider what this says about the church and about our attachment to the past at the expense of the present.

Many, perhaps most, of Jesus' followers were young, as many of those who have been prophetic have been. Perhaps their very youth allowed them to live more by trust and passion, and less by a conviction of their own wisdom and strength. Remember the Lord speaking to Jeremiah: 'Do not say that you are too young.' There are no barriers to discipleship. The young Jesus called young people. The church must recognize both that calling and the fact that it will not necessarily show up in the ways we think it should. The young Jesus does not need to be protected by us, but perhaps he sometimes needs to be protected from us.

Iona Abbey, September 1987.

4
The Living Tree

John 15.1–17

On the first Sunday in Lent, I walked into my home church in Glasgow, and stopped still as if the breath had been taken away from me. I saw that up in the sanctuary, the cross which had been brought in to be the one we would use in worship throughout the whole Easter season, and would decorate with daffodils on Easter Day in celebration, had been made from the tall Scots pine Christmas tree we had decorated for the festival of the incarnation two months earlier. It had not been smoothed down, it was still the rough bark, and growing from a few branches that still clung to the trunk were green pine needles, sweet with the smell of the forest. I can hardly find words to describe the visceral depth of response I had to this cross; all I know is that I found myself rooted there, saying 'yes' with all of my being, while around me, people tried to squeeze past to their seats.

Later, I knew that the 'yes' had come spontaneously to my lips as an unforced response to a new recognition of the living tree. I remembered the words of the fifteenth chapter of John's Gospel: 'I am the vine and you are the branches, remain in me, and I in you, for without me you can do nothing.' I knew that I was looking at the life without which I can do nothing. And simultaneously, I knew I was recognizing my connectedness to all living things, through which the same life flows, and saying 'yes' to that connectedness also. It was a sacramental moment.

Several weeks later, I had the great pleasure and privilege of working with a group of twelve women – Catholic, Methodist, Episcopalian and Presbyterian – whose ages ranged from twenty to late sixties, who had come together from five local churches to create Stations of the Cross for a Good Friday liturgy in St Mary's Cathedral, as part of the local ACTS (Action of Churches Together in Scotland) group Easter celebrations. We had spent a lot of time just talking, sharing experience, hopes and fears, getting to know one another, confessing what felt like our artistic and theological inadequacy to complete this task, and working together on the fourteen visual representations of the way of the cross. We encouraged one another, panicked at different times, finished the last station fifteen minutes before the service was due to start, and had to change our plans several times. At 7.25 p.m., we were still not too clear about who was doing what in the liturgy. Then, as we began, as poem flowed into prayer, as prayer flowed into song, as the candle was lit before each station, and the taper passed from hand to hand, as we moved round the church and well over 100 people moved with us, I knew it would be all right. I did not have to worry. And so it was. We had learned to trust one another, to overcome our differences and be sensitive and responsive to the demands of the task in hand. But more than that, we had learned to trust our connectedness, and the life that flowed through that. As we moved round, it was not so much that we were imposing a structure on the event. It was more as if that flow, that life, was carrying us round, and we were trusting enough to respond. We had got in the flow; we were remaining in the living tree and bearing fruit. It was a sacramental moment.

Last week, I had the very interesting experience of working with two groups back to back, one an all-male group, the other an all-female group, both of just a few people. When I arrived to join the group of men, I discovered that their mode of working was a critical, dialectical and at times fairly confrontational one. This was an intellectually rigorous process, sharp, challenging and demanding. Long ago as a theology student in Glasgow, one of a handful of women among over 100 men, many of whom were deeply hostile to women in ministry, I had become fairly adept at this mode of working. Now, as then, I find it a mode that is initially quite attractive. It has a high adrenalin factor, it is stimulating, even challenging. But it is a way that contains its own dangers. As a student, in order to survive in this mode, I had learned to split off my ideas and beliefs from my tender wounded soul, constantly under attack as I found myself. It was a form of protection – but a damaging one. It took me years to repair the

damage, to heal the splits to the extent to which they had happened. Now, I am not as tough as I used to be, and I have learned
to see this as a good thing. And, because I know it is easy for me
to revert back to a critical, even polemical mode, I have learned
to seek other ways of working. As the time with this group, who
had been working together for some months, went on, I began to
realize once again that I was operating in ways I did not like about
myself, and to realize that I was feeling increasingly bruised.
Eventually, I got to the point where I expressed this feeling.
Somewhat to my surprise, other members of the group suddenly
began to share the same feelings, to express their needs and their
hurts. It was a painful time.

A little later, one of the men in the group, rueful and a little
angry with himself, said, 'We men are so bad at taking care of
each other.' It seemed to me a hopeful sign that more and more
men are beginning to acknowledge this, to name it unprompted,
and not simply to dismiss such feelings as weakness too threatening to share. It was a sacramental moment.

The following day, I was doing some work with a group of
women returners to the job market. In contrast to the previous
group, this one was open, vulnerable, ready to share its struggles,
its failures, its worries. The connectedness was clear – they had
a strong sense of their mutual inter-dependence and need of
support. And yet, in this group of women, many of them single
parents, most of them managing on low incomes with more skill
and flexibility than they realized, resourceful and creative, there
was an underlying and pervasive note of insecurity, of lack of
belief in their own abilities and strengths. A rigorous critical
perspective would show that, in spite of a prevailing culture that
conspired to make them feel inadequate and their aspirations
negligible, these were strong and competent women with a huge
amount to offer. At the end of the meeting, one of the group said,
'What we need is someone to come in and tell us about all the
good things we have done and can do.' This too was a sacramental moment.

I don't want to suggest that men by nature are more confrontational, and more dependent on putting a brave face on things,
fearful of admitting weakness. I know how adept I can be at
doing that. Nor do I want to suggest that women by nature are
more open to admit vulnerability, and to get in the flow, the sap,

of connectedness. I have known too many men who have taken great risks to do just that. What I *am* talking about are processes that teach people, women and men, to behave and react in particular ways. We all need a critical, rigorous process in our work and our lives, we all need to submit ourselves to the pruning Jesus talks about in John's Gospel – it will help us to bear more fruit. But if it is abstract, theoretical, if it is separated from our equal need for connectedness, for care, for taking care of one another, then it becomes bruising and eventually brutal. Without the connectedness, the remaining in the living tree, our spirits, we ourselves, wither up and die.

And perhaps it is that the road towards discipleship of equals has two branches: the first, of recognizing and affirming our connectedness, our membership one of the other; and the second, of recognizing and disciplining and pruning our strengths, to bear more fruit. These two paths need each other, and we need to be sensitive, as Jesus was, to which one people are on at which time. To those who knew very well how to admit woundedness, who knew their need, poor people, some of the women he met, sick people, foreigners, those crippled by their past failure, his words and actions said, 'Get up, stand tall, you are also strong, there is a place for you to listen and learn and teach and be heard and be valued. Your experience is important, your knowledge matters.' To those who depended on their strengths, who were fearful of showing weakness, who affirmed themselves through rigid dogmatism and confrontation, he said in his words and actions, 'Humble yourselves, you are weak, stop being separate, distant, see your connectedness even with the worst of sinners.' And he took on the role of a servant, and washed his disciples' feet.

Getting in the flow, trusting our connectedness, requires that we open ourselves to power. Not power as the world knows it, but the power of the Spirit, the power of the living tree, and that can be scary for those accustomed to living in powerlessness. It requires a lot of trust to be open to the power of God. We need one another for courage. But equally, it takes courage to let the power go out of us, to admit weakness and vulnerability, to open ourselves to power-sharing and redressing balances. In the story of the woman with the issue of blood, Jesus felt the power go out of him when she touched the hem of his garment. But instead of panicking, armouring, attacking back, as so many people do when they have to relinquish some measure of power, Jesus was happy to let it go, to allow the woman to be empowered, because he knew that his source of power was not limited, did not depend on him, was inexhaustible. It is the difference between *power over*, which, held on to, is about control and status and fear and insecurity, and is abusive, and *power to*, power to act, to do something, to realize potential, which is liberating.

It was the power of the living tree, the sap of life, which must decrease and die in order to increase and live and bear much fruit. We are called as disciples to bear much fruit. To be equal sisters and brothers in discipleship requires that we encourage one another, use our gifts in one another's well-being, and open ourselves to new ways of understanding power and powerlessness. We need pruning and we need connectedness. We need sacramental processes that allow that to happen. We are branches of a living tree.

Melrose, Ecumenical Decade of the Churches in Solidarity with Women, Mid-Decade Service, 24 April 1994.

5
Passion, Sap and Grace

Are the churches spiritually dead? It's a premise supported by a great many people, and not all of them hostile to the person and teachings of Jesus. And yet, in the very framing of the question, it is possible to see grave symptoms, if not of actual morbidity, then of a kind of terminal decline. Perhaps it is a particularly academic or clerical trait, from a tradition accustomed to the severance of theory from practice, so comfortably to separate and hold apart, as if it made perfect sense, two aspects of being which have no meaning, and indeed no existence one without the other. I refer of course to the spirit and the body.

For, after all, what *is* our spirituality other than our profoundest motivations, our deepest desires, those longings, instincts, intuitions, insights and dreams, which animate us, breathe through us, move us and inspire us, and which we value and prioritize subsequently according to our cultural conditioning, our belief systems and our life experience and concerns.

And where does that spirituality find expression, become realized, show up, except in and through the physical, in our bodies, in the flesh? Do we touch with anything other than the surface of our skin? Can we move without activating a complex interplay of bone and muscle and tissue? Can we be in relationship with our environment except through a highly sophisticated range of sense perceptions? Does our brain function from somewhere other than from within our skulls? You can take a child at birth, attend to basic feeding functions, but if it is deprived of all tactile contact, if it is not held, stroked, hugged in any way, it will be seriously damaged, may even die. The body needs to be loved to live, and for the spirit to live. It is this integrity of body and spirit, and the valuing of whole people, spirit and flesh, that I take to be the deepest meaning of the incarnation of Jesus Christ, the embodiment of a different value system.

'The physical is the only arena for the expression of holiness', said George MacLeod. Because holiness is only possible through the physical, however we pretend otherwise. Such a pretence only makes us strangers to ourselves. When bodies are alienated, tortured, starved, beaten, armoured or in other ways not cherished, the spirit shares that fate, suffers too, and though the human spirit has the capacity to endure and transform very great suffering, there are many whose spirits are tragically and profoundly damaged by such suffering. There are people whose spirits are dying because their bodies have been assaulted, because their labour is deemed redundant, because their colour is described as ugly, because their gender is called inferior, because their age is thought weakness, because their culture is seen as ignorant, because their pain is belittled, because their lives are made expendable over and over again. George MacLeod also said 'If there is a spiritual problem, you have to ask, what is the matter', what material issue is not being addressed. To know about the spiritual health of the church, it is perhaps necessary to concentrate on bodies. And here I am not talking symbolically. I'm talking about the church's relationship to actual physical bodies.

When I think about bodies, and about what I find lively and vital and attractive in people of all ages from babyhood to extreme old age, there are three qualities I find most characteristic – passion, grace and what I want to call sap. By passion, I mean an openness to and a love of life in all its fullness, what the Bible means by the word *suffering*, meaning allowing, bearing. By grace, I mean the capacity to appreciate and thence to be generous, even extravagantly so. By sap, I mean a sense of connectedness running through all of life, even to its extremities, even as a green tree is full of sap. But it can seem often as if the church, at least institutionally, has little passion, grace or sap.

Of course, this tends to be a natural consequence of acting as if we are dead from the neck down. In our over-cerebral church culture, the word becomes not flesh but more words, theory is all too often translated into more theory. Martin Luther said of theology, that discipline of discovering a story to live by, 'A man does not become a theologian by understanding, reading and speculating, but by living, by dying and being damned.' (And perhaps a woman too.)

In our worship also, we are all too often dead from the neck down, static; we don't move, enthusiasm is suspect, the display of grief an embarrassment; we sit far apart and our symbols point only back to themselves, to another service, not to life. There is nowhere for agony and nowhere for ecstasy. Why is so much 'Christian' music, art, theatre so desperately dull? Is it because it always has to conform to predetermined agendas, and lacks any sense of real risk, of being on the knife-edge where prayer becomes real?

And as for sexuality: 'There goes a man who thinks it wrong to be immoral. Being immoral means having an orgasm with anyone you are not married to. Or even wanting it, though wanting it is not as bad as getting it' (Sidney Carter). The church is terribly stuck with a reputation of being at worst deeply anti-sexual, and at best wanting to tame and sanitize and control that which has life only if other possibilities are recognized and integrated (though not necessarily acted upon). But it is hard to do that if you can't be honest, and the penalties for honesty in the church can be ferocious. Sometimes it will crucify anyone who reminds us of these things we know about ourselves but prefer to attribute to others.

But if the church is not honest, then where can we go when we are struggling with the fact that there are also other things that we want, conflicting desires, contending values? We set up committees and working parties on this, that and the next thing, but when anyone seems to have come too close to all the messiness, ambiguities, agonies and ecstasies, then they are ruthlessly excluded. The last thing we want is to get too close to the mud. After all, some of it might stick.

As with our sexual bodies, so with the body politic. Politics, economics, journalism are all dirty, messy, nasty things. If we get involved, we might be compromised, be theologically incorrect, have to argue our corner, fight to stand. Much better to keep our hands and our noses clean, let them get on with it, stand on the side-lines and fire poisoned darts. Unemployment, war, hunger, huge injustice and corruption, well, we can pray about it, take up collections, stick plasters on the ailing body of the health service as it is assaulted. It's all a far cry from the passion, grace and sap of the Scots Confession of 1560: '. . . the works which are counted good before God . . . to save the lives of the innocent, to repress tyranny, to defend the oppressed'.

Meanwhile, people bleed to death, and we worry about the mess on the carpet. But it is our life-blood too. The church in this country is not dying of persecution or hostility. The sickness doesn't come from outside. Nor is it cruel or bad people within it. The body is being suffocated and starved by its own relentless niceness. We want nice buildings, nice clergy, nice hymns in church, and we do a special line in nice girls. It's a place for nice Christians.

But where do you go if you don't feel nice? What if you feel like hell, what if you feel fury, despair, fear, lust, humiliation, vengefulness, loneliness? These are not nice; we would rather you just took them quietly away somewhere else. They are not acceptable. So we pretend to be nice, and move further and further away from reality. It is very uncomfortable not to be nice. But that hard place is the only place we grow, outwardly and inwardly. So we choose not to grow. We entropy. We run down.

I sometimes get the impression that the church in Scotland doesn't really believe that we are saved by faith. Here, we are justified by being good, which translates into being nice. We're not even very good at enjoying our misdeeds – and if we can't enjoy them, what purpose do they have other than to relieve us occasionally from the burden of relentless niceness. So the great thing becomes to avoid displaying any sign of weakness or flaw or vulnerability, and to patronize, or worse, despise those who do. You mustn't be caught, not even by yourself. We are strangers to ourselves. And to others. No passion, no grace, no sap.

If we are afraid to name, own and assume responsibility for our profoundest motivations, our deepest desires – because they are carnal, material; because they show up in the body, in all their ambiguity and power and terror; because we have been taught to suspect them and be afraid – then we have no possibility of creativity of imagination, no ability to take risks, wander in strange worlds knowing that even there we are God-encompassed. Salvation does not consist of the severance of the spiritual and the material, but in their reconnection at deeper and deeper levels. 'Love is not concerned with whom you pray, or where you slept the night you ran away from home. Love is concerned that the beating of your heart should kill no one' (Alice Walker).

Without the ability to imagine, even just for a few moments, what life looks like seen through another's eyes, without the capacity to empathize with the pain or delight of another, to know that *there have I been, and there I am,* without the courage to go beyond the boundaries of our own self-interest, prejudices, cares, needs, and meet others without defences, how can we affirm, with Paul, that 'if one part of the body suffers, all the other parts suffer with it; if one part is praised, all the others share its happiness' (1 Cor. 12.26)? It is not just that we *have* bodies, we *are* a body, in which the divisions are the illusion and the barriers and the disease. Of all the divisions, the most damaging is that of one part of ourself from another part of ourself. As long as we are strangers to ourselves, then we will be deeply strangers to others. Sometimes it may be our experience of being deeply loved by another that can bring us home to ourselves; sometimes it is our experience of deeply loving another that will bring us home. Life is kinder than we let it be, for there are so many occasions for love, if we don't let fear overpower us. So many opportunities for healing, for wholeness, and all of them signs of the grace of God that desires to go on loving us and healing us and calling us home to ourselves and to each other. But without the facing of fear, even stumbling, even trembling, even sick to the pit of our stomachs, without these abandonments of jumping off the cliff into the arms of God, then we can only armour, repeat, retrench, self-protect, and whine at anyone who is different from us. And face lives without passion, without sap, without grace.

Some of you may have seen the film *Shirley Valentine*. There's one scene in it where Shirley, a woman just beginning to come home to herself after years of stagnation and separation, is being made love to on a boat in the middle of the sea by a passionate Greek fisherman. Suddenly she becomes embarrassed by the thought of him seeing the stretchmarks on her stomach from her pregnancies, and in an agony of self-consciousness, she starts to pull away from him. But he will not let her be embarrassed, tells her that she should not be ashamed because these are the marks of experience, the marks of life. And then he kisses them.

Of course, you could say it was just a good chat-up line. But in the cinema where I saw the film, people cheered.

The last thing the church needs is purges, enemas, disinfectant. Unless it can embrace bodies, can kiss the marks of life, it is dead, and only the rattling bones of its corpse remain, discarnate, unburied and unhallowed.

Adapted from a speech given at Glasgow University Union, January 1994.

6
For Free

Luke 15.11–32

When my children were small, like many children they were very keen on Postman Pat. In one of the books, *Postman Pat's Rainy Day*, there is quoted the phrase from Matthew's Gospel, 'The rain falls on the just and the unjust alike.' For some reason, the children found this phrase hysterically funny, which I suspect may have had more to do with their understanding of the word 'just', than with a deep appreciation of the divine sense of humour. For a while, Duncan took to marching around the house proclaiming in a loud voice that the rain falls on the just and the unjust alike, which was rather an unnerving experience for any adults who happened to be around.

But I don't find it surprising that children should instinctively like the idea, given as they are to the same extravagant gestures of love as that of the rain falling on the just and the unjust alike. 'I love you best in the universe' or 'I want to give you a million kisses' seem neither illogical nor unnatural things for children to say.

We adults, however, are more inclined to be suspicious of extravagant love, gratuitous love. We have a tendency to expect results for it, not perhaps in the more obvious ways of being thanked, or of getting something in return, but in the sense of there being something to show for it – a person changed, a situation improved, a wrong rectified. And when these things don't happen, as is sometimes the case, then there is occasionally the feeling of having squandered our valuable love, thrown it away to no purpose, of having failed to get a suitable return on our investment.

25

Extravagant love can make us feel terribly uncomfortable, even threatened. It's not so bad if we can see that extravagant love directed towards something less personal – towards nature, or great art, for example – but then, perhaps in these instances we do get some kind of return on our investment: a beautiful landscape will never disappoint; Mozart or Rembrandt or Shakespeare, or whatever your taste is, will never fail to please.

People, on the other hand, will often let us down, fail to please us and we them. The sting of hurt and injustice are very real, and so we can perhaps sympathize with the Prodigal Son's elder brother in his feelings of outrage at his father's extravagant love. It is such a familiar story, of the reckless younger son, squandering his inheritance in riotous living, ending up on the streets, coming home humiliated and ashamed to throw himself on his father's mercy. And finding, before he has ever said a word, his father out to welcome him with open arms, and planning the party to end all parties. So familiar a story, in fact, that we can sometimes overlook its offence, the scandal of this story.

For in it, Jesus showed more clearly and simply than in any lecture or sermon the radical difference between his message and the teachings of the tradition in which he had been raised. For the moment, let the elder brother stand for the way of the law, the way of doing the right thing, the way of duty and good deeds, of hard work and faithfulness. And let us remember that there is nothing wrong with any of these things. We, all of us, rest on them every day of our lives.

Then let the younger brother stand for all those whose lives are very different, all those who are irresponsible, feckless, immoral, outcast – the kind of people Jesus spent such a lot of time with (and took the flak of respectability for doing so) – criminals, cheats, thieves, drinkers, prostitutes and the like. By the tenets of the law, by what we might call a kind of natural justice, what such people deserve is punishment, retribution, their come-uppance, their just deserts, the cold shoulder. Why, there are some, like the younger son, who don't even have the excuse of a deprived upbringing. They have no excuses. But what they actually get in Jesus' story is something very different. They get the open arms of love. Not for Jesus the separation of people into deserving and undeserving. In fact, he went out of his way to seek out the so-called undeserving. He didn't wait for them to come to church. He went out looking for people who were prodigal.

Well, I ask you, what kind of society would you have if you went around showing extravagant love to bad people instead of giving them the kind of punishment the laws of good and bad require? This is a very revolutionary idea, is it not – not one to be encouraged at all, now, as then? But nevertheless, it is how Jesus understood the nature of the relationship of God towards human beings. We are unconditionally and extravagantly loved, whoever we are, whatever we have done. This love is not something that can be owned or achieved. It is a state of being to be realized and acknowledged and celebrated. It is gift, absolutely free, gratuitous. It is a love which is offered whether we are good or not. It does not depend on us being morally good. It is not conditional.

Does this mean, therefore, that there is no such thing as judgement? Or that justice is simply an illusion? Or that the law of right and wrong might as well be done away with? Or does it mean that people can just go on being corrupt and cruel because it doesn't make any difference anyway? Assuredly not.

Let's go back to the story. Remember how the younger son wasted and squandered his inheritance, spending his money trying to buy friends, spending it using women as things, not persons. And how, when his money was all gone, there was no one around to treat him as a person, not a commodity to be bought and sold. He brought judgement upon himself. Under the judgement of law, we reap what we sow. He lived refusing just and right relationships to others, and in turn they were refused to him.

And there he might have died, under judgement. Except that something happened. He came to his senses, the Bible says. He had a realization. He realized how well, in contrast, his father treated people, even his hired workers. He realized his father's love. And the moment he realized that, he became aware of the great distance between himself and his father. They were separated by a huge gulf – not by his father's choice, but by his own. *He* was the one who had wandered off into a far country. His father had not gone away, his father was still there. And simultaneously, he became filled with a huge desire to go back to his father, to present himself in all his weakness and failure, exactly and openly as he was, and throw himself on his father's mercy.

The writer Janet Morley, in her book *All Desires Known*, a title taken from the collect which begins 'Almighty God, unto whom all hearts be open, all desires known, and from whom no secrets are hid', comments on that phrase, 'all desires known': 'it is . . . an appalled sense of self-exposure combined with a curious but profound relief'. We have probably all felt that at some time or another – the need to name and acknowledge our weaknesses, hurts, regrets and hidden longings, and the hope that they will be accepted without condemnation, even with love. We can certainly see it clearly in the prodigal younger son, that appalled sense of self-exposure, of vulnerability, of nakedness – and yet the curious but profound relief at putting down the burden of defiance, of self-justification. 'Here I am. This is me, no pretences.' We can see the hope beyond hope that his father would accept him, at least as a hired hand. And so he sets out to close the vast, self-imposed distance between himself and his father.

This coming to his senses, this realization of love, this desire to be accepted in all our nakedness and woundedness, the church has called conversion. The word conversion literally means to change and go in a new direction, and it is a good, precise image to describe the move away from separation and towards that from which we have separated ourselves. But it is not an urge which is impelled by law. If he had been relying on law, the prodigal son would never have turned. It was the realization of love that got his feet going. Law cannot bind us where we don't want to be bound. It can only give us a devil's choice between breaking the law and its subsequent imprisonment of judgement, or the more subtle imprisonment that binds us with invisible chains through fear of punishment. The father could, we suppose, have refused his son his inheritance, forced him to stay at home. But, a wise parent, he knew that love forced or coerced, even by the demands of law, is not love at all. So he set his son free, free to make his own mistakes. There isn't a parent who has not suffered love this way. And yet we know we have to let our children go, we have to let them grow up, and be separate and assume responsibility for their own lives.

And the Prodigal Son, realizing the extent of his father's love, came home. He found that he had not realized the full extent of that love. It went far further than he could ever have imagined. He came home to welcome and acceptance and delight in his return, before he had ever uttered a word of repentance. But his older brother wasn't very happy about any of it. He'd been good. He'd done his duty. No one had ever had a party for him. He was very aggrieved. Well, we've all had that feeling too, haven't we?

'You ought to love him less. He's no good.' 'You ought to make her pay. She's been bad.' Like the elder brother, we want to make the father in our own image. We want a small God, to fit in with our small minds. But we can't have that. God is always wanting to break open the limitations of our hearts and minds and make them bigger, inviting us to expand our knowledge and understanding and experience of love. The elder brother shows so clearly the limits of law – and the cost of these limits. It is easy for us to slip into a kind of legalism in our faith: if we are good, we will win God's love and favour, be rewarded; if we are bad, God will punish us. But we don't have to win God's love. We already have it. We simply have to realize it, accept it. Not, of course, that it is in fact at all simple to accept what may fly in the face of everything we have been taught to believe, implicitly or explicitly, to the contrary. There are many messages we need to refuse in order to accept this very different one. But if we *can* accept that we are loved unconditionally, then, subtly, our desires shift, to a desire to live *in* that love, and to live it *out*. We desire what is true and loving not in order to be loved, but because we are loved. There is a whole world of difference between these two.

You are always with me, said the father to his older son. Everything I have is yours. Perhaps sometimes we get so driven by the need to be good, to do our duty, that we forget that it's also all right to be happy, to be extravagant, to do enjoyable things just for the pleasure of them, to delight in the gifts of life. God will not take them away from us because we're enjoying them. Perhaps God would prefer it if we enjoyed them more. We might be more generous with others if we were more generous with ourselves; more generous with love, with laughter, with friendship, with creativity. God does not ration these things. They are limitless.

And perhaps it would then be easier for the older brother part of us to be generous to the younger brother who is also in all of us, more ready to admit our weakness and need, more ready to admit the envy that often fuels our self-righteousness. God doesn't limit us to a choice of being bad and happy, or good and miserable. God offers us freedom and healing, acceptance as whole people who come bearing the marks and wounds of life. God offers us, all of us, life in all its fullness, no tricks, no conditions. We just have to say yes to that fullness of life. But we can only lay hold of it, realize it, when we accept it's also on offer for everyone else.

In hot, dry, dusty, water-parched Palestine, rain does not come as the miserable curse we sometimes experience it as in cold, damp Scotland. In Palestine, it comes as the bringer of new life and growth, as sweetness and refreshment and delightful coolness. It comes as blessing. And it falls on everyone. For free.

Lansdowne Church, Glasgow, 6th Sunday after Pentecost, 1993.

PART TWO

Justice, Peace and the Integrity of Creation

7

Linking Lives, Trading Places

You've just been made redundant. Your company, a big multi-national, needs to maximize profits for the benefit of its share-holders. So they're taking their business to a part of the world where labour is cheaper. Your skills, your increased productivity and those of your workmates are no longer needed, and the large amounts of public money which have been paid out as an incentive to investment are simply written off.

On the other side of the world, let's say in a rapidly industrializing Asian nation, you've just got a job. A new factory is opening up. They like the opportunities here. The weak currency gives them a good rate of exchange, and the lower standard of living means that they can pay lower wages than in the Western country where they were before. Because there are very few union rights, they don't have to worry too much about over-long working hours, or tight safety measures or environmental safeguards. You know that your working conditions will be lousy, but you have little choice. You have a family to support, no social security, and few chances of improvement. Chances are you're a woman.

You're a British miner. You've just heard that your pit is scheduled for closure, and that your whole industry is being virtually shut down. You produce good quality coal in safe conditions that your father and grandfather suffered to get. And your output has increased consistently over the years. But the country can get cheaper coal from elsewhere – including from places where desperate men live apart from their families most of the time in order to get work in the mines. And anyway, you know the rhetoric – you can't buck the markets.

Or let's go back in time a little. You live on the land, and make

33

a frugal but sustainable life from it, and you belong to a community which is almost like an extended family, whose leaders have always defended your interests in return for your loyalty. But now your leaders, whose life-style has been moving further and further away from yours, and now requires a level of wealth to sustain that is simply not possible for all of you, have decided that there's a more profitable use for the land you live on than having it peopled. They have discovered what would nowadays be called a cash crop – one which can be marketed for money. It's called sheep. So they are going to drive you off your land, burning your homes over your head, pushing you out to starve or freeze, brutalizing your family and, in the process, breaking every tie of honour and loyalty that you've always held sacred. And they will use all the institutions of society – state, education, even church – to justify what they are doing, so that it's you who are seen as the problem. You are left with some very unpleasant choices. You can huddle round the fringes of the Atlantic Ocean, trying to make a bare living from fishing and beachcombing. You can take your family and move to the rapidly growing cities to live in squalid slums and work in soul-destroying factories. Or you can get on a boat, endure weeks of disease, misery and storm, and try your luck in a strange and hostile land. And then you can do to the native inhabitants of these strange lands what has just been done to you – move them off their land and destroy their communities and culture. This process will come to be known as the Clearances.

All of this will be very familiar indeed to a woman called Rigoberta Menchu, a Guatemalan Indian who this week was awarded the Nobel Peace Prize. Because it is her story as well – with one important difference. Her people have been pushed off their land on which they grew their food by powerful and rapacious landlords. Her people have been oppressed, starved and brutalized when it suited the needs of profit. Her people have been imprisoned, tortured and murdered when they attempted to resist. Her own father, mother and brother were among the 100,000 people who have died in Guatemala in the last twenty years.

Let's go back to the one important difference. Our economic system, which now has the entire world in its stranglehold, is called free-market capitalism. It purports to allow the markets, that is, people's consumer wants, to regulate production and distribution, and the same markets to sustain both the profits and losses of such a policy, and to bear the costs of it. But the wider picture is not quite such a simple or pleasant one. Some people share the profits. A larger number sustain the losses. And the largest number of all bear the costs, because this whole policy is based on a system of what we might call externalizing the costs, making someone else pay. During the Clearances, the landlords did not bear the costs of land clearance. The people who were cleared bore them, and the far corners of the globe to which they were scattered bore them. In the sweatshops of Asia or the coffee plantations of South America, the costs are not borne by companies or landowners. The costs are borne by the poorest of the poor. In the West we have grown rich by being able to export our problems – our landless people on to someone else's land, our nuclear testing into someone else's atmosphere, our acid rain over someone else's forests, our dangerous products, from weapons to baby milk, into countries that cannot afford them, do not need them, and from whom we extracted the raw materials in the first place.

But for Rigoberta Menchu, and for the millions like her across the world, there is nowhere left to externalize the costs to. No North America, Southern Africa, Australia to sail to – these doors are firmly closed to people who are, like the Scots were 100 years ago, economic refugee migrants. There is no way of flight. The only option left for them is to fight, to fight an unjust and demonic economic system that sacrifices human beings in their millions on the altar of economic theories. In the vast continent of Africa, bearing the burden of debt from the time when the West encouraged huge borrowing from its oil surpluses, International Monetary Fund and World Bank policies are causing misery on an enormous scale – famine, disease and the destruction of health and education services. And in this world disorder, we are all involved, we all participate. The effects are beginning to be felt, even in Britain. More and more we are seeing the true nature of externalizing the costs, making other people pay for our comfort.

This is not the way of Jesus Christ. We preach the cross and the resurrection. We believe in a God who so loved the whole world (not just our little part of it) that he sent his son to show us what it means to love, even to dying for love. Each of us, in our own way, have been touched in our lives by the grace of that God of love. And because we are human, we want to be cheerful and optimistic, to think everything will be all right. But we are dancing on a precipice. We are singing into the teeth of a rising wind. Underneath our feet is a world which is cracking under the weight of its own injustice. The wind that is rising is the breath of a thousand million people who have no voice and no choice and nothing to lose when they howl in sorrow or anger or despair.

I do not much want to think about the injustice of the global economic order which allows so much hunger and want in a world of plenty, so much needless suffering and squalor in a world of great material and human resource, so much lack in the midst of so much abundance. I do not want to think about the fact that my life is supported by an economic undergirding in which I have a complicity. There is so much about my life which is blessed and good, that is creative and fulfilling and life-enhancing. Therefore, it is hard to admit how much of that which I take for granted is enabled by the suffering of other people. But I must admit it. I must think about it; I must let it address my life. If I do not admit it into my reality and make it part of my truth, then I carry within me a belief and a vision which are fatally flawed, and ultimately death-dealing.

My belief is not a unique one. It is a belief in the values of love and justice and care, embodied in the particular person I am, in attempting to work out what it means to be loving in my relationships, a good enough parent to my children, caring towards my neighbours, responsible as a world citizen within a particular country. It is a belief in the goodness and integrity of all created life, in the call of each individual to growth and delight in creativity, in a communal life that supports and encourages all within it. It is also a belief in a life-giving God, in Jesus who liberates us, in the Spirit which empowers us. It is a belief in laughter and tears and touch and change and kindness, in the value of forgiveness. It is a belief in others. It is a belief in myself. As I say, it is not a unique belief.

But it cannot only be a belief for my sake, or for my family, my community, my country. It must be a vision that extends to everyone. If I say that this is really only possible for some people

– the educated, the enlightened, the caring and concerned, the Christian – then in truth, what I am accepting is a belief in expendability; that there are some people for whom life in all its fullness is not worth working. Expendability has taken some monstrous shapes this century alone – Auschwitz, Hiroshima, the gulags, Cambodia. But if I accept the expendability of the poor, the landless, the nameless, the powerless, by my actions or my failure to act, then I am also accepting the underlying assumptions of fascism and totalitarianism, and rejecting the gospel of Jesus Christ, for whom every single person was beloved and precious and valuable.

Therefore, because I want to love God in the *whole* of creation, I must admit the injustice of the world economic order into my reality. I must see its upholding and maintenance as a major factor underlying wars, political alignments, the arms race, neo-colonialism and many forms of oppression, racism and sexism. I must see that it makes the hill-farmer in Thailand, the child prostitute in the Philippines, the landless labourer in Brazil, the migrant worker in Europe, the uprooted homeland dweller of Southern Africa, the starving refugee in the Sudan part of my life and my interdependence, and my responsibility. I must do some trading places, some linking of lives.

I am realistic about my life. I did not, and nor, I hope, would I, choose the present economic order. I was born into complicity with it, and I have benefited from it. Being an educated white Westerner, I am one of its winners. So the sins of the fathers are visited upon the children. It would not help anyone, would be self-indulgent for me to attempt to carry all the guilt of complicity upon my shoulders. There is no point in wringing my hands over what I am not responsible for. Guilt should be reserved only for what I am responsible for, which is my *continuing* complicity. My permission was not sought for what exists. I do not need to go on giving my permission for injustice. I may choose to dissent, to say I beg to differ. There are always ways in which I can refuse to give my permission for injustice.

Nor would anyone be served by my refusing to pursue what is good and beautiful and truthful in life, even though few may benefit, even though I am aware of the inadequacy of what I do. Justice bereft of love and delight is, in the end, arid, just as love which does not incorporate justice is, in the end, self-indulgent and self-defeating. So I must live with the tension of witnessing to the good and beautiful, while also engaging in the struggle against the ugliness of hunger and poverty and oppression.

How can I live this tension? All that I have power over, and have the right to have power over, is my own life. So I may begin at the most basic level, and try to live a way of life that includes personal economic responsibility and sharing, and avoids over-consumption and the lures of consumerism. What that means for me is a matter of reflection and honesty and humility. And I can be politically engaged as a citizen, and avail myself of all the rights I have, which for me are far less limited than they are for many others, to engage with the political processes that shape economic decision-making. To do less is to betray all the people who do not have the same rights, and depend on all of us to exercise ours on their behalf. To do less, whatever the shape of my political engagement, is to keep silence in the face of injustice; and silence, said Nadezhda Mandelstam, is the real crime. To speak out matters, makes a difference, but what matters just as much, perhaps more, is to listen to those whose voices are often unheard because they are weak or poor or powerless. And to listen, we have, sometimes at least, to draw near to where people are, to trade places, to link lives, to remember that it is not they so much as we, comfortable and secure, who are the problem.

Our Lord Jesus creatively embraced the tension of justice and love, and was a powerful advocate for the poor and voiceless. Following him, we are led into responsibility towards all people. In his spirit, our affirmation of life is renewed and deepened. Amen.

One World Week, 1992.

8
The Love of Money

We brought nothing into the world, and we can take nothing
out of it; but as long as we have food and clothing,
let us be content with that . . .

The love of money is the root of all evils, and there are some
who, pursuing it, have wandered away from the faith,
and so given their souls any number of fatal wounds.

(1 Timothy 6, 7–8, 10 Jerusalem Bible)

'Money is everything', said Gore Vidal, American historian and
political commentator on a British chat show recently. Perhaps he
is familiar with this comment from George Kennan, Head of US
Planning during the restructuring after the Second World War:

> We have about 50% of the world's wealth, but only 6.3% of its
> populations . . . our real task is to devise a pattern of relation-
> ships which will permit us to maintain this position of disparity
> without positive detriment to our national security . . . we need
> not deceive ourselves that we can afford the luxury of altruism
> and world benefaction . . . the day is not far off when we are
> going to have to deal in straight power concepts.
>
> (Paul Baker, *Song in High Summer*)

America, says Vidal, does not any more elect its presidents and
senators. Running for political office is so costly that now politicians are hired by financiers and defence interests. The 'money
boys', George MacLeod calls them, and is well known in the Iona
Community for his insistence that until we confront them, the
unjust economic status quo will continue, despite all our best
efforts of charity and concern.

Whether we accept the 'politicians for sale' theory for our country or not, money is, if not everything, then a very great deal in Britain just now. A Chancellor's resignation, soaring interest rates, the European Monetary System, flurries on the stock-market and the changing economic strategies of the Labour Party – these are the issues that, more than any other, determine political priorities and personal finances. And not just for the British. Interest rates change, share prices fall, and the machinist in Taiwan and the miner in Zambia are as affected as their counterparts in Port Glasgow or South Yorkshire. Church and community celebrations of One World Week are simply stating the obvious – we are, whether we want to be or not, one world.

And, therefore, as we approach that great sales and marketing opportunity sometimes known as Christmas, this seems like an appropriate time for *Coracle* to think a little about money and our relationship to it. 'The love of money is the root of all evils', says 1 Timothy, and certainly, some of the things that have been done in pursuit of wealth make a very convincing argument in favour of original sin. Curiously, though, for such a strong biblical statement, these words have been somewhat ignored by many who have a great dedication to other parts of the Pauline canon (on personal morality and the role of women, for example). Perhaps that's because it's still quite socially unacceptable to say that we love money – we are 'creating wealth', or 'realizing our assets', or 'protecting our interests', or 'investing in the future'. If we don't actually love money, but only what it can do for us, then there's no theological problem – or at least, it's someone else's problem.

And it's certainly that. Western economic policies, sometimes known as development, have signally failed the countries of the Third World. And the cost of failure, the burden of foreign debt, which affects almost every country, from South Africa making political manoeuvres in an attempt to reschedule its foreign debt, to China tripling its debt in one year, describes the reality of being born into bondage in Ecuador.

People's innate sense of justice and fair play leads them to see that 'something is rotten in the state of Denmark'. But we need a framework, a story, to give us words of advocacy. The biblical story is of sufficiency – discerning what is 'enough' is an ongoing task. And we need practical beginnings to help us translate our sense of wrongness from despairing paralysis into political will.

These reflections do not constitute our last word on money, or on the complexities of global economic policy. They barely scratch the surface. And Christians are often accused of naïvety in our economic thinking – too much woolly talk about 'sharing', and 'life-style'. But as all the old idols topple, 'development', 'socialism', 'privatization', 'enterprise', and as our free-market economy teeters on the dungheap of environmental disaster and profound human suffering, perhaps we need to re-evaluate the naïve clichés, and give them firmer flesh. Otherwise, our Christmas celebrations of the Word become flesh are tragic indeed.

Coracle, *Winter 1989.*

9
Women in Demand

Women are in demand. Nothing new about that, you might think; women have always been in demand; or at least, they have always had demands made of them. But the nature of this present demand, which is for a major increase of women in the labour force, caused by the decline in the birth rate, means that it might just be easier for women to negotiate the terms under which they work from a stronger position than they are used to. For although women already make up almost half the workforce in this country, they still labour under considerable disadvantages when compared to men. UN statistics state that half the world's population is female, they do two-thirds of the world's work, own one-tenth of the world's wealth, and own one-hundredth of the world's land. Things may not be quite so bad in Britain, but it is still the case that equal pay for equal or comparable work is far from a reality, and equal opportunity (by which is meant not only access to education, training, advancement and leadership, but the ability, through encouragement, confidence, freedom from discrimination and changing social attitudes, to take advantage of that access), is even further behind. The present government has brought in legislation to extend access through changes in the tax system. It remains to be seen whether they have the same commitment to enabling those presently disadvantaged in employment opportunity, who also include black people and people with disability, to benefit from that access.

But though the future may look brighter for women, there are also grounds for caution. History demonstrates that it has been all too easy for women to make great progress and then suffer great set-backs. Women in Scotland (for example), enjoyed far more freedom fifteen hundred years ago than they did five hundred years ago. And curiously, it has often been at times of so-called enlightenment that they have suffered most. The French Revolution was closely followed by the introduction of the most fiercely repressive legislation for women in history, the Napoleonic Code. And a look at today's world confirms just how fragile many hard-won rights for women are. So it is important that we are familiar with our history, especially where it has hidden or forgotten the part played in it by women. That it is still vital to remember the past is borne out by the fact that Lesley MacDonald was recently invited to contribute an article for a forthcoming dictionary of church history and theology (in Scotland), a project which has been under way for three years. Out of a text of 650,000 words, she was offered 1,000 to assess the contribution of women in Scottish church life. So are women marginalized. That situation has been rectified, but it is a warning against complacency.

And we would do well also to be cautious about the nature of the work offered to women. Do women really want to be 'the best man you have' (as Mr Reagan said about Mrs Thatcher). It is a spurious freedom which offers the opportunity to join a competitive, confrontational and individualistic work ethos. A questioning by women of what they are being wooed to join would do both men and women a service.

As would a revaluing of the whole concept of service. The servanthood of Jesus is the model of discipleship for Christians, especially enjoined upon those who would be leaders in the church. But this has always been a hard one for men in the church (especially its leaders) to follow. Though there are those who would suggest that the problem of too few men is really the fault of too many women (especially when women seek a more equitable representation in leadership, as might befit a 70/30 per cent split), might the cause not really be the difficulty that men, conditioned to expect service, have with the notion of servanthood.

The concept of mutual service between men and women is a necessary consequence of more women working outside the home. That there is little progress to mutuality is borne out in studies which show that women still bear the double burden of jobs and domestic responsibilities. Yet the consequences of this unequal division may well be felt in the increasing breakdown of family and community life, and the victims our children. For most women, including women in the church, there is no going back to the (relatively short) time when men had jobs and women stayed at home. Social mobility, the death of the extended family, better education for women, and above all, the sheer pressure of economic necessity (and the vast majority of women work because they need the money, such is the cost today of housing and raising a family), have made lifelong domesticity a lonely and frustrating option for a great many women. The questions that changing social patterns raise are for men as well as women, and men have a lot of catching up with women to do in addressing them. A change to greater mutuality is a hard one to make (I speak from experience) but ultimately rewarding for everyone, men, women and children. Mutuality takes everyone seriously.

Most of us are so concerned most of the time with the business of simply being human, that the political and personal implications of gender seem irrelevant, overstated, or simply an argument about the ring round the bath. In that respect, our lives are sheltered from that society where women receive ten million obscene phone calls each year, where many women are afraid to go out of their homes at night, where women and children are raped, battered and threatened, where the responsibilities of fatherhood are consistently abnegated. Our society. But just because we don't suffer, or perpetrate, does that mean it's not our problem?

Coracle, *Spring 1990.*

10
Life Together

Removing all trace of racism from our relations means
affirming that we are different, and that we
shall remain different.

(Edgar Pisani)

All over the world there is an explosion of difference going on.
Since the dramatic events in Eastern Europe last year cracked the
Berlin Wall down the middle, and one after another the Eastern-
bloc countries threw off the straitjacket of state communism, the
West has watched in amazement, delight and some trepidation as
people have once again affirmed their right to be different. They
have proclaimed loud and clear the right to differ from conformity to an inefficient and corrupt single economic theory. They
have proclaimed the right to differ from conformity to the
exhausted political ideology which sustained the theory, at the
expense of the very well-being and security it purported to seek.
And they have proclaimed the right to differ from conformity to
an imposed and imperialist culture, and to affirm their own distinctive cultural and spiritual values.

Nor is this explosion of difference confined to Eastern Europe.
In every continent, resistance is growing to solutions imposed
from above, from outside, from over there (wherever over there
is perceived to be). Confidence is growing in Southern Africa
that the time is not too far off when people of different races will
have the freedom to determine for themselves how to live and
where to live in their own land. In Palestine, the Intifada (whose
literal meaning is something like 'the shaking of the founda-
tions') is not simply the frustrated reaction of an occupied people.
It is the carefully planned infrastructure of an emergent state; it is

the decision to be different, made by people who are no longer content to conform to other people's images of controlled dependency, whether these images be Jewish or Arab.

And even here in the United Kingdom, ten years of economic policies perceived by the majority of Scots to be culturally unacceptable (of which the closure of Ravenscraig and the death-knell of the Scottish steel industry are merely the latest), have led to an increasing sense of the need to affirm Scottish difference, both politically and culturally.

Like everything in life, this explosion of difference is both good and bad. It is good that people, even after years of repression and suffering, still say, 'we shall not die, our distinctiveness will not be lost to the world in the way that so much natural and human distinctiveness has already been lost'. It is good that here and elsewhere, there are questions, there is resistance, to plans and programmes for 'development', be it for nuclear dumping, the erosion of green-belt land, or Sunday ferries, which threaten cultural survival.

But the dark side of difference is starkly seen in the violent ethnic conflicts breaking out all over Europe (and breaking out with most force where difference has been most rigidly contained). It is seen in the ugly spectre of anti-Semitism rising once again over Europe. It is seen here in Britain in crass and repugnant comments about who you support at cricket, and in anti-Scots or anti-English chauvinism. Everywhere on earth where difference is affirmed, the racism that excludes, oppresses, or attempts to obliterate difference is also seen.

George MacLeod once wrote, 'Only a demanding common task builds community.' Christians affirm, not individualism and not collectivism, but persons in community. The Oxford Dictionary gives as its first definition of community 'joint ownership', and here, of course, we are reminded of the truth that though different, we are destined to share the one earth. Unless and until we find ways of living together while affirming our differences, ways of building community, white with black, men with women, Israelis with Palestinians, Azeris with Armenians, Protestants with Catholics in Northern Ireland, then we are all doomed to a senseless and increasingly bloody cycle of action and reaction.

In the demanding common task, two imperatives, among

many others, present themselves for Christians. One is that unity in difference, persons-in-community, is only possible where justice and equality are guaranteed for all, including minorities. State communism has signally failed to do this, and has subsequently collapsed. Free-market capitalism, by definition, is incapable of delivering justice and equality. Therefore, this demanding common task presents itself to all people of goodwill.

And secondly, we are living in times when the symbolic has never been more important. The symbolic is that which unifies, the diabolic that which severs and divides. The symbols of Christian faith point to persons-in-community in a comprehensive and inclusive not exclusive way: the Trinity, God in community of difference; the body of Christ, broken to be shared out in community; the cross, the resurrection of the body; the Madonna and Child, the community of God with humankind. Christians embody these symbols in their lives, and they are resources that allow us to affirm that people are different and will remain different, but may nevertheless be engaged in the demanding common task of life together.

Coracle, *Summer 1990.*

11
Angry at the Church

'There is Hope', proclaims the Church of Scotland's rainbow slogan on the side of Glasgow buses. Well, perhaps not, according to Tom Torrance, former Church of Scotland Moderator, retired academic and well-known theologian. In a sustained polemic in *Life and Work*, the Church's magazine, Professor Torrance describes what he sees as the 'alarming collapse in private and public morality over the last 20 or 30 years' and lambasts those 'political and public churchmen' whom he sees as directly responsible for this alarming state of affairs.

There are, of course, many ways of seeing our society, and these tend to depend on how we experience it directly. The single parent, for example, whose existence is cited as an example of the degradation of society, may feel that it is a step forward that domestic violence (by no means a new phenomenon) does not have to be a life-sentence any longer. And others would argue, and would even have evidence to support their arguments, that adultery, incest, child abuse, pornography and prostitution have not so much increased as been recognized as having widely existed in the past, but in a context of complicity, cover-up and hypocrisy which did not allow of their victims' suffering being assisted. In the Victorian era, when the biblical teaching that moral law and natural law are closely interrelated had more lip-service paid to it (is this the time Professor Torrance believes we should return to?), child prostitution, drunkenness, teenage vagrancy and domestic brutality were the huge sore on the backside of public and private morality, along with the endemic poverty that bred them.

The Editor of *Coracle*, having been a teenager in the 'Swinging Sixties', and therefore, according to Professor Torrance, one of the 'young people starved of spiritual nourishment, who yielded to the appeal of erotic pop music designed to induce and heighten wild emotional states in which moral restraints gave way to rebellion, sexual promiscuity, drunkenness, drugs, suicide and the occult' has different memories of that time. She remembers a time when young people protested against the hypocrisy of a standard which claimed the high moral ground while ignoring the napalming of children, the profiteering in weapons of mass destruction, and the relentless pursuit of a standard of living which could only be attained by the impoverishment of large parts of the world. And she remembers being inspired rather by churchmen and women who refused to countenance the dehumanization of other human beings on account of their race, class or sex. And she remembers a church life characterized, not by any desire for 'popular relevance'; but by a humble and faithful desire to love God, whom we cannot see, by loving our neighbour, whom we can see. And a quest to seek out what it means to live in righteousness, in right relationship with friend and enemy alike, without the easy resort to simplistic clichés and platitudes.

If we believe that Christian faith is indivisible, and that indeed the incarnation is central and controlling in our church life, both individually and corporately, then we must surely regret that preaching private morality is so often seen as a substitute for practising public morality. The two belong together, and sniping from ivory towers at committed Christians who are doing their utmost to discern the will of God in the marketplace, where family breakdown, political powerlessness and real and grinding poverty are exacerbated by an irresponsible and privatized public ideology is not helpful. The last thing such endeavours need is a privatized church. And calls to return to a golden age which, in truth, never existed, are a dangerous irrelevance to divert us from seeking real guidance and direction for the real problems that face the church in the present and for the future.

Problems such as living creatively in the tension between the understandable desire of many that the church should be a haven of security and continuity, a safe and loving sanctuary in the midst of loneliness and insecurity; and the belief that the church should also be constantly changing and reforming, moved by the Spirit, turned around in conversion, sent out in mission, living in the upside-down kingdom, lighting up dark places and charting new paths. What does it mean to be both sanctuary and light? And what are the ways to 'touch the hearts of all' that the Spirit is directing us into in Scotland now? Are they simply more of what already exists, trying to do better what was done in the past, but with dwindling resources, and a clergy who are stretched almost to breaking-point? Or is the time upon us to take some risks of faith? The Church of Scotland, for example, is committed to a much greater mutuality of ministry between clergy and laity. But in order for this to happen, both groups will need to be liberated from the unreal expectations of the other, and the church will need to address its latent hostility to the idea of teamwork. Otherwise, too many faithful Christians will go on being angry at the church.

Coracle, *Winter 1990.*

12
The Taste of Honey and Bitter Apples

There is a well-known lager commercial which manipulates our deepest desires with its skilful use of symbols. It depicts a people in bondage, pushing a huge weight up a steep hill, and ends with the weight being pushed off and the people breaking loose in an anarchic liberty. The caption is 'Free the Spirit' – in this instance, the pinnacle of human aspiration is a pint of lager.

Nevertheless, it is a powerful piece of communication, addressing us at a number of levels of our being. For, in the horrifying aftermath of the Gulf War, it feels as if 'all of creation is groaning with pain'. The agony of the Kurdish people is echoed by famine in the Sudan, devastation in Bangladesh, fear and suspicion in the Soviet Union, homelessness in Britain, and the anguish and bitterness of countless smaller, but no less real, bloody conflicts. Even the earth itself is groaning in burning oil wells, poisoned lakes, scorched earth, and other kinds of 'collateral damage'.

And for people of faith, living after Easter, resurrection is experienced as shot through and through with pain. Robin Ross, writing on the Middle East, expresses this perfectly in a memorable image of new life – a taste of honey and colocynth (bitter apples). Sweetness and bitterness together.

This is our experience as we savour the sweetness of the liberation of Kuwait – but taste its bitter aftermath; as we savour the sweetness of a home of hospitality – but taste the bitterness of those who are homeless and hopeless in London.

To live in the risen life is to be fully alive to life in all its fullness. Therefore, it is to suffer, in its original meaning 'to allow', the passion of life. And to transform that suffering into victory through the discipleship which addresses us with the eternal Word, calling us to respond in the here and now, with love. We incarnate the Word in our lives, and it becomes our flesh, moved to care and to act.

At the moment of Jesus' death on the cross, the temple veil was ripped from top to bottom, and the heart of what Jewish identity meant, the symbol of the covenant relationship with God, was laid bare to the world. In that moment of self-surrender, of abandonment and despair, the love that suffers even death tore away the last reservation and offered a new covenant, fulfilling the old, to the whole creation. For on the resurrection morning, the love that suffers was also revealed as the love that saves.

Dying we live. And, as we see how principles and patriotisms, our other-loves and our self-loves lead only to further anguish when we exalt them to the status of idolatries, we are confronted once more with the cross. Apart from the love that suffers, there is no security, no safe harbour. But this love of God accepts us, embraces us, forgives us, and confronts us. This love will carry.

And by it, we are brought into right relationship with God. The movement of eternal dying and rising is seeing the glory in the grey.

And yet . . . will it always be the case that we must crucify Christ afresh, before our hearts of stone can be melted into hearts of flesh? Right relationship with God and self must eventually extend into right relationship with others. We do not fully experience Easter in our lives until we also experience Pentecost.

The Spirit moving within us, driving us towards God, is also inviting us into communion with others. And in this dialogue of life is the energy that enables transformation of relationship, that empowers. As John Taylor has said, '. . . the Spirit's power operates always in the interactions of community rather than in the recesses of the individual soul.'

Pentecost did not happen the day after Easter. Perhaps resurrection takes a bit of getting used to. Instead, the disciples waited, and prayed, and held an election. And suddenly without warning, they were filled with power, and were able to understand each other's language. In these dark days of 1991, filled with huge preventable suffering, we look for the freeing of the Spirit. We pray for the peace of the world. We ask, give us a Pentecost again. And, like the disciples, we cannot predict where or when or how the Spirit will move among us. But we can wait in hope and readiness, open to its coming. This is not a passive waiting, but the active expectancy of the peacemaker, breaking down barriers, taking the risks of peace upon ourselves, making room for the movement of the Spirit.

Once again we are back to the love that suffers. Some words of prayer of George MacLeod seem appropriate ones at this time:

> If love does not start with us, it will never start at all. Pentecost is not some future hope. The rushing, mighty wind of peace is howling to get in the shuttered fetid prison we have contrived, buttressed by our prejudices, barred and bolted with our fears. Give us faith in peace again, faith in your way of peace. It will only come from you to each. It can only come through each of us right now. Take the terror from us. Give us faith.
>
> Or, failing that – give us the honesty not to pray to you for peace at all.

Coracle, *Spring 1991.*

13
The Way Ahead

At the time of a General Election (and indeed, for many months before) political parties, pressure groups and pundits of every description and affiliation attempt to convince us that their blueprint represents the way ahead, and that they alone can lead us to a better and brighter future. At the same time, other voices sound what is both a warning and promise, reminding us of what has always been the wisdom and intuition of people of faith – that the way has less to do with where we are going and more to do with how we travel. And indeed, that how we proceed will determine where we eventually arrive. So, we find that there is a contradiction between massive programmes of privatization in many areas of life and the demand for public responsibility; between the continuation of the Trident build-up and the stated desire for nuclear de-escalation and peaceful disarmament; between peoples who feel that their cultural distinctiveness and political aspirations are neither heard nor honoured and a dogma which is more inclined to respond 'but we know what's good for you'. In so much of British life, the inconsistency between means (ways) and ends is glaring and shameful.

To walk, even for a little way, with others is to remember that we are also on the journey. If, as Oscar Wilde said, 'once at least in his life, each man walks with Christ to Emmaus', it is also the case that once at least, everyone comes with Christ to Jerusalem. And, if we do not always have choices about finding ourselves confronted with its crowds and dirt, its poverty and conflicts, its intrigues and power-struggles, we still have choices about how we will walk its streets. The fourteen Stations of the Cross are a traditional form which, usually pictorially, retrace the steps of

Jesus on the Way of the Cross. The way of faith is only, ever, one more step, and then another, and then the next one.

For many, many people, struggling with racist immigration laws or official indifference, with mental health problems, with violently oppressive political and economic structures, or simply with the complexities of being human, it is often darkly unclear where Christ is leading. It is the faith of all the great religions, and of revolutionary humanism, that just and merciful means will ultimately bring about just and merciful ends. But it is the resurrection promise and hope for followers of Jesus (of whatever place, time or belief) that seeking to walk how he walked, not denying the cross in that, makes us participants, not just onlookers, in the doing of the will of God.

. . . let us pray

that we may see the way to the cross
and the way beyond it.

Help us, Lord
to follow where you walk
to stop where you stumble
to grieve where you die
to dance where you rise again,
knowing that this is the only way.

There is no other way.

(John L. Bell)

Coracle, *Winter 1991.*

14
Knowing Where We Stand

There is, of course, a great deal more to the agonizing and bloody conflicts raging like a fire out of control through Eastern Europe (not only in the hell of Bosnia, but also in the less-reported countries of the former Soviet Union, and potentially at least, in half a dozen other places) than questions of national and cultural identity. Whatever the rationalizations of ethnic autonomy or cultural self-assertion, there is an underlying question of basic human values. How we are able to answer the question 'What does it mean to be a Serb alongside Bosnians or Croatians (or indeed, a Scot alongside an English or Irish person)?' will depend on how we answer the question 'What does it mean to be a human being alongside other human beings?'

There are plenty of reasons to be found for the present tragedy of the former Yugoslavia: years of repression and militarism; the arbitrary drawing of boundaries and equally arbitrary displacement of whole populations; the enormous social and political and economic problems left in the aftermath of the Second World War; grievous injuries from the past never given the chance to be admitted and healed, but instead simply covered over and left to fester; painful memories never reconciled but instead buried ready to emerge when finally given space; Western promises made and never kept; mob psychosis and a climate of violence. Plenty of reasons which have led to the point where one young woman could say, 'For years, they were our neighbours, now they are cutting our babies' throats.' But reasons are not the same as excuses. There is no excuse, no justification for the torture (of language as well as of people) of the lie of 'ethnic cleansing'. There is no excuse for slaughter, destruction, theft, intimidation, cruelty and the abuse of power, no matter who is doing it. The fact that everybody has reasons for doing it does not constitute an excuse. And this is a tragedy in which West and East have a dreadful complicity. We are all involved.

Nevertheless, because we can see the dangers, because we have been and still could be there, questions of national and cultural identity must be taken very seriously. Whether we like it or not, a sense of place and of culture, a sense of belonging or not belonging, is a crucial and influential part of human identity. Land and people exert a powerful emotional hold on us. If we feel insecure in these, or if we perceive them to be under threat from some quarter, either internal or external, we are more likely to be aggressively defensive, more likely to demonize 'outsiders', less able to respect and value the gifts and wisdom of other cultures. There are intimations of this in the relationship between Scotland and England, not in outright hostility, but in a kind of sulky resentment, in the kind of jokes and comments which, directed against any other race would be deemed racist, and in a self-pitying whinge that is not keen to admit any Scottish faults or failings.

Many, perhaps most, Scots believe that the relationship between Scotland and England would be improved by greater self-determination for Scotland. Members of the Iona Community have been part of this movement.

Many, perhaps most, Scots have felt the relationship with England seriously threatened not just by questions of national autonomy but by the espousal of an individualism during the Thatcher years that does not sit comfortably with Scottish communal and public values. The liberation theologian, Jon Sobrino, has defined spirituality as 'profound motivations'. Whether these more communal values are really the profoundest motivations of Scots needs further probing, and if they are, do we, in common with those English, Irish and Welsh people who share them, have a spirituality that will help us resist their erosion?

Coracle, *Summer 1992.*

15
Coming to Birth:
A Labour of Love

1992 has been a year which, in many respects, seems to have been characterized more by death than by birth. The keen hope of something new coming to birth out of the collapsing communist regimes in Eastern Europe has grown bitter amid the welter of confusion and fear of many countries: resurgent racism and anti-Semitism in Germany, deep symbolic and constitutional division in Czechoslovakia, turmoil and destruction in the countries of the former Soviet Union, and the bloody agony of what was Yugoslavia. Africa too, seems like a dying continent, ridden by war, famine, poverty and drought, where even the earth itself appears to collaborate with death. And in a Britain sunk in recession, two observations present themselves. We appear to be witnessing the demise of public accountability and honour, the complete paralysis of the ability to assume responsibility for the consequences of decisions (which in itself deals a grievous blow to the capacity of language to convey truth). And this is happening in no small measure to prop up economic systems that are death-dealing – either directly, as in International Monetary Fund conditions for debt rescheduling in Africa, or indirectly, as in the squandering of billions of pounds in the vain effort to stave off withdrawal from the Exchange Rate Mechanism.

When structures and institutions appear to be in terminal crisis, it is an act of faith to seek out the continuing signs of birth and creativity, and to affirm these, and, for now, it is easier to see them on a smaller scale, as salt, as a million pin-pricks of light rather than a massive illumination. But they are there, wherever people, sometimes in the most appalling circumstances, choose to respond creatively rather than destructively, and struggle with love to bring life and meaning and care out of the enormous constraints within which they operate. And to do so requires the exercise of choice, because such creativity does not just happen. It is the product of pain and tears and hard labour, like any birth. Perhaps one thing that can stand as a sign of choosing life is found in the liberation of courage, care, insight and love among so many suffering from or affected by the AIDS virus. In the midst of hatred, fear, vilification and death, the positive response of many is inspiring and humbling.

This Christmastide, *Coracle* seeks to celebrate life and creativity, in story, poetry and image. These are not a retreat into escapism, or a flight from the anguish of the world. Rather, they are the creative effort to give form to the human hopes, motivations, hurts and insights that all of us share. They represent a creative reflection and action, which is found in daily service of others, in political engagement and protest, in all love given flesh. They are a symbol of saying 'yes' to life against all the odds.

Last month, Trident finally came to the Clyde. As dissenters gathered weeping at the sight of this death-dealing instrument, the Iona Community's Justice and Peace Worker, Helen Steven, paddled a canoe into the path of the oncoming vessel. Pulled out of the way by Marines who were 'saving her life' (their words) at a point where her own affirmation of life was so strong that it confronted her with her own death, she said later that she thought people felt her to be foolish and foolhardy, and part of her was inclined to agree with them. And perhaps in worldly terms she is foolish. But the message of Christmas is that Christ did not come among the powerful and privileged, and the Word of God took human flesh in weakness and folly, small, unprotected, and ready to suffer for love. *Coracle* wishes all its readers many labours of love and many joyful births this Christmas and in the coming year.

Coracle, *Winter 1992*

16
The Culture of Violence

The world watches in impotence and horror as former Yugoslavia bloodily dismembers itself, and debates whether to arm or not to arm, to intervene or not to intervene.

In Russia, as the old order is cast off and power struggles are waged, the cost of change becomes more obvious, and more threatening, as it is in Germany, and other countries of Eastern Europe.

In Britain, a number of particularly horrific instances of violence against children begin to bring home to more and more people the undercurrents of fear and hostility and disintegration in our society.

And in Scotland, workers at Rosyth wait nervously to discover whether they will still have jobs, refitting nuclear submarines, or whether the work will go instead to Devonport; and workers at Kvaerner in Govan celebrate a huge defence contract, but workers at Swan Hunter on Tyneside lament, because Govan's gain is their loss. These issues in the news are not, of course, unconnected. They have one striking feature in common. They all require the existence of an enemy. All of them might name and describe the enemy in different ways, with different labels.

They all require the enemy to justify their own actions. If you have a theoretical enemy, then the end can justify the means. But a closer examination shows up a very different, and disturbing, common factor. Whatever or whoever the theoretical enemy, they all have the same actual enemy.

At the point of delivery, the target is the same. It is always the weakest, the most vulnerable, the most defenceless in any society. In the culture of violence, human relationship is grossly distorted.

Powerful people, institutions, societies, paint themselves as the victim, and so are able to justify the naked abuse of power. But reality is that the victims are other.

Children are the victims of the violence of adults. Women are the victims of the violence of men. The aged, the very young, the sick, are the first and greatest victims in war. These same people bear the brunt of economic policies designed to protect the interests of the successful – poll tax, water privatization, VAT on domestic energy.

There are millions of low-paid or jobless people in this society who experience their environment as hostile, as likely to mount assault after assault upon them. And our political processes, however laudable their goals, all too often operate on the principle of the end justifying the means. They are processes for winners, and by their very nature, they exclude those the culture of violence, the culture of survival of the fittest, consigns to its own valuation of bad housing, no jobs, and social disrespect. This *Coracle* explores the assault on the poor, globally and locally; the effects of the arms trade; the nature of poverty as a violation of human rights.

Poor people are not truthfully defined in terms of lack or deficiency. A culture of peace, of right relationship, values processes that do not divide human beings into losers or winners, but show the richness and fullness of life and faith of many we are accustomed to thinking of as failures.

Coracle, *Summer 1993.*

17
The Centre and the Edge

Brian Keenan, for five years a hostage in Beirut, was recently being interviewed on television. He had come home, he said, much richer after his experiences, than he had been before. An extraordinary statement by a man who had returned from years of incarceration, isolation, abuse and assault which had brought him to the edge of madness. And yet his book, *An Evil Cradling,* is a vivid demonstration of how one man, his life stripped down to the barest essentials, pushed to the extremity of existence, not only survived but transcended his limitations in an affirmation of common humanity – and so was enriched, and enriched others.

You don't get much more marginalized than in a Beirut prison. But that voice from the margins – powerless in worldly terms, pushed beyond our imagining – spoke as so many people speak from the margins, prophetically. Pushed to the edges of society by a dominant centre, squeezed out of employment, education, health, decent housing, or out of participation, community, acceptance, respect, or out of land, citizenship, freedom and even life itself, the marginal voices are many. Sometimes the voices are loud and strident, and we choose not to hear them because we don't like the way they speak. They're too disruptive, they use bad language, they challenge the status quo aggressively. Sometimes the voices are faint, almost inaudible, the voices of people who have been told to 'shut up' so often that their throats have nearly closed up. But we fail to hear them, even if we have to listen very attentively, at our peril, and to our impoverishment.

Because in these voices from the edge, we are hearing people who show us the possible future. Up against a wall, whether it be the wall of poverty, exclusion, war or stigmatization, blocked from going forward, blocked from a way back to the centre, people, if they are not utterly defeated, discover or create ways to survive. Some of these ways may be fierce, violent, the re-emergence of old and terrible strategies that have been long submerged. But some of the ways are genuinely new, innovative, hopeful.

Which ways will triumph, the old terrors or the new possibilities, will depend at least partly on the willingness of those at the centre, those with security, acceptance, opportunity, power, to listen to the voices from the edge, stilling fear for long enough to affirm common humanity and a common struggle.

Coracle, *Winter 1994.*

18
Something Whole

Jesus said: No one can enter the Kingdom of God
unless she is born of water and the Spirit. A person is
born physically of human parents, but is born
spiritually of the Spirit.

(John 3.5–6)

This morning, in a little while, we are to celebrate the sacrament
of baptism. So I want to talk about what a sacrament is, and
about the meaning of the sacrament of baptism in particular.

Sacrament is a word we hear quite a lot without necessarily
understanding quite what it means. We know that the Church of
Scotland describes two activities, that of baptism and that of
communion, as sacraments, but when we think about these two
activities we tend to concentrate on what actually takes place
– with the water, with the bread and wine – and on their individual meanings, rather than on what the two have in common.
What is it about them that means we describe them both as
sacraments?

The word 'sacrament' actually comes from two different
words of Greek and Latin origin. One of these words means *holy,*
and the other word means *mysterious.* The Catechism describes a
sacrament as 'an outward and visible sign of an inward and spiritual grace'. So a sacrament is something which is both holy and
mysterious, something which is sacred and yet in some way hidden from us, beyond our understanding. As we know, the word
holy simply means *whole*: it suggests that which is complete,
perfect, undivided. When we talk about the holiness of God, we
are saying that God is one, indivisible. The Holy Trinity is a way
of saying that God is made known to us in different ways: as

Creator, the giver of life; as Immanuel, God among us given human flesh in Jesus Christ; as the Spirit of holiness who moves among us, renewing us and connecting us one to another. Yet though made known to us in different ways, God is not divided, God is holy, whole. Muslims recognize this wholeness when they say in their profession of faith, 'God is one'. And when we in our turn strive for holiness, we are also seeking wholeness – the wholeness of not being divided from God, the ground of our being; the wholeness of not being divided from our fellow creatures on this earth; the wholeness of not being divided in our own lives where our words say one thing but our actions communicate another.

Similarly, a sacrament might be thought of as something – an activity, a moment, an event or experience – which demonstrates this quality of completeness, of wholeness, of being undivided. It is, if you like, a little bit of heaven on earth, an intimation of life that is lived in God-likeness. Because heaven is that state in which what is incomplete will be completed, while encompassing incompletion, where what is broken will be healed while encompassing brokenness, where what is empty will be filled up while encompassing emptiness, where what is separated will be united while encompassing separateness, where opposites and polarities will be held in a greater unity. A little bit of heaven on earth, a promise of what we long for and yearn for.

And yet in its very holiness, there is a mystery. We do not understand why this moment rather than another should be so blessed. We do not understand why we should get this blessing. We cannot put our finger on exactly what is going on. We can simply receive, and enjoy and be grateful. Its exact nature is mysterious.

The word that the Christian church has used to describe this experience of heaven on earth, this holy thing that we do not understand, is the word 'grace'. We believe that the grace of God is at work here. Here, too, it is important to give attention to the meaning of words. The word 'grace' is, above all, something which is pleasing, something in which we can take delight. Yet the same Latin root from which it comes also carries the meaning of thankfulness, of gratitude. *And* it carries the meaning of something which is entirely free, for which no payment is required. It is gratis, for nothing. So grace is pleasing and delightful, *and* it is freely offered, *and* the response appropriate is one of wholehearted thankfulness. These intimations of heaven are gifts of grace that come generously to people who don't know why they are being given, and aren't too sure of whether they deserve them, and are sometimes a little hesitant about accepting them. But the gospel message is that these gifts of grace are offered even to those who believe that they are utterly beyond the reach of hope or grace. There are none too lost, too despairing, too doubting, to be beyond grace. Even in death, grace is there.

Of course, we do not only experience the grace of God in the sacraments of the church. We experience grace in many ways and in many conditions. In that sense, all of life is sacramental, for in all of life we find, often where we least expect, occasions when the grace of God is communicated to us. I spent the last few weeks in Israel and Palestine with a small group of Scottish church people, including the Moderator of the General Assembly. The tragic killing of twenty-one Palestinians and the injuring of many more took place at the Temple Mount in Jerusalem the day we flew home. So, as you can imagine, my thoughts have been very much in that city, and with that land and its peoples. I have found myself walking down Great Western Road in the rain, but have seen instead of grey skies and traffic and red sandstone tenements, the cloudless blue skies of the Galilee, the slow-moving donkeys of the Jordan Valley, the labourers in the vine-yards and the flat-roofed Arab houses festooned with grapevines and surrounded by drooping olive trees.

On our visit, we saw many things we would rather not have seen – refugee camps running with open sewers, little girls on their way to school lined up against a city wall in Jerusalem by soldiers, teenage soldiers of both sexes with rifles slung casually over their shoulders as our teenagers would carry a guitar or a tennis-racket. We talked to many suffering and driven people: those who had seen their dreams of a new life and a new freedom go sour on them; those who felt that their dreams of going home would never come true; those who were too weary and too beaten to have a dream at all. And yet, in the midst of this agonized land and its divided people, there were also many sacramental moments; moments of holiness that were so full of the grace of God that I could only say helplessly to myself, 'I have done nothing to deserve this'. I think of occasions of wonderful hospitality when people who were complete strangers, Israeli and Arab alike, spread feasts before us, and opened their homes and their hopes to us; of visiting the Sunday School of the Greek Orthodox church in Kafr Yusif, a village in the Galilee, and watching literally hundreds of bright-eyed eager children shout out the answers to a Bible quiz; of gazing out from a balcony high over Nazareth on to starlight and a sleeping town, and catching the scent of pine and eucalyptus; of sitting in silence in an open-air chapel on the shore of the Sea of Galilee; and of evening worship in a Benedictine monastery on the road to Jaffa, listening to the most beautiful plainsong I have ever heard. So many meetings, people, places, so many not just archaeological remains but living stones, keeping alive their faith in the most difficult circumstances. In all of these, God was present, the moment was complete and whole and holy.

But there are two memories in particular I would like to share with you. One is of visiting a refugee camp called Jalazon in the occupied West Bank. Here, in the most stifling and repressive conditions, about 6,000 people attempt to maintain family life and community against all the odds. We had spent the afternoon visiting nursery schools and a women's centre, and walking the streets, being shown the bulldozed and sealed-up houses. Now we had been invited to the home of a woman whose 13-year-old son had been shot dead. There were about ten of us, sitting in this bare and utterly impoverished household. Yet even here, the duty of hospitality had to be observed. I saw the bottles of lemonade being passed in the back window from where I was sitting, and in a minute all of us were graciously served with refreshing glasses. We were sipping our drinks appreciatively because it was very hot and dusty, when suddenly there was a loud crack followed by another. A minute later, an elderly man rushed into the house, choking and spitting, and then the tear-gas began to drift into the room, making us cough and our eyes smart and run. We had to put down our drinks and move into an inner room, and then, hurriedly, out of the house and back to our car, just as a fully armed army patrol came racing down the hill towards us. There was disarray, the moment of hospitality and the sharing of grief was shattered, and the women who were our hosts were distressed and embarrassed – for our sake, because for them this was a regular occurrence. A moment of grace was terminated in fear and confusion. I experienced this as a diabolical moment, a moment when things fell apart. This is how we recognize the force of evil at work in the world – it causes things to fall apart.

The second memory was particularly meaningful for me, because it made a connection between Glasgow and Jerusalem. Those of you who have children in Hillhead School may know the Zatar family, who have been living in Glasgow for three years. They are Palestinian refugees, Mrs Zatar from the Galilee, Mr Zatar from East Jerusalem. Mr Zatar's elderly mother and some of his twelve brothers and sisters still live in Beit Inan, a small village on the outskirts of Jerusalem. But he has not seen them since 1967; he is not allowed to enter the country, and though he had the correct papers when his father died in 1984, he was not allowed even then to go home to attend his father's funeral. A week ago today, I visited Mr Zatar's family home in Beit Inan, was welcomed in their house as if I was the queen, took greetings from their son and brother in Glasgow, and took some pictures of a family not seen for twenty-three years, including new nieces and nephews. Many tears were shed and much excited conversation took place through an interpreter, because I can't speak a word of Arabic. You may be interested, as I was, to know that this village is the traditional site of Emmaus. I believe that in this Muslim family, who called down every blessing of God upon me, my children, my friends and my church, I encountered Christ in the stranger's guise. When I got back to Glasgow and took the photographs round to the Zatars' house, both of them wept, in joy, but also in sadness that a foreigner could do what they could not – visit their families. The shattering of family and community is another sign of the diabolic – things fall apart.

On Thursday, the Zatars returned to Jordan, and to an uncertain future with their four children. So the tragedy of the Holy Land touches us even here. It is a reminder that it is a terrible thing to threaten and damage the gift of grace, whoever or wherever that threat comes from, and to whomsoever it is directed. It is to spit in the face of God. Of course, we don't often mean to do this: we do it unawares. All the more reason, then, to walk with humility, and to listen with sensitivity around those concerns and hopes and occasions which are precious, those times of love and hospitality and friendship, of family and community life, of vulnerability and closeness, of confidences given and trust received.

The opposite of the diabolic is the symbolic, that which brings or draws things together, that which unites. And baptism and communion are the sacraments, the holy and mysterious activities of the grace of God, which our church recognizes as symbolizing and pointing to our unity with God, and with one another in faith. In baptism, which simply means bathing or sprinkling, we are grafted into Christ as a member of his body. In communion, as the body of Christ, we both share in his life here and now, and are guests at a table which is the foretaste of the great feast of life God prepares for us.

So we approach these sacraments with the same humility and sensitivity with which we should approach all sacramental moments. Today, Caroline Lynsey Honeyman will be baptized into Christ's church, not as a junior or apprentice or temporary member, but as fully part of the body. She will be a member of us, our sister, and we are called to know her in that way. If she suffers, then we share her suffering; if she is happy, then we share her rejoicing. In baptism, she will be buried with Christ; in baptism she will be raised with Christ. The diabolic power of all that shatters and divides and forces apart will be defeated by the symbolic power of the sacrament of God's grace, which unites and completes and defeats all that annihilates. Caroline was born whole and complete, she is already loved, by her Creator as well as by her family. Baptism is not about remedying some terrible defect in a tiny baby, nor an insurance policy against the pain and struggle of life. But it is an invitation to an extraordinary deepening and an extraordinary dimension of human life, to the fullness of life lived connected to God and to all creation that comes to us through life in the Spirit. And so she is born again, of water and the Spirit, not just to her humanity, but to her divinity also. We who are her spiritual family are required to nurture the fullness of life and potential in Caroline, and to be a kind of cradle wherein she may not be divided against herself, but be whole. In this task, which is ours for all of Christ's body, including each other, we are encouraged not only by baptism and communion, but by countless sacraments of grace which are freely gifted to us. Let us cherish these gifts, and seek to preserve them from all that causes things to fall apart.

Lansdowne Church, Glasgow, 19th Sunday after Pentecost, 1990.

19
Transfigured by Ceremony

The church has always been most powerful when the material and spiritual givens of existence have been closely interwoven. In the Middle Ages, for example, it was able to exert such a hold on people because its teachings addressed the questions of day-to-day life which were a mystery to ordinary people. And the power of the medieval church was not primarily that it offered explanations, but that it had awesome ways of symbolizing the deepest questions of human existence.

The Orkney poet, George Mackay Brown, has written:

> It is ceremony that makes bearable for us the terrors and ecstatics that lie deep in the earth, and in our earth-nourished human nature. Only the saints can encounter these realities. What saves us is ceremony. By means of ceremony, we keep our foothold in the estate of man, and remain good citizens of the kingdom of the ear of corn. Ceremony makes everything bearable and beautiful, for us. Transfigured by ceremony, the truths we could not otherwise endure come to us. We invite them to enter. We set them down at our tables. These angels bring gifts for the house of the soul.

The power of ceremony

All cultures have had ceremonies that made truth, so far as it was understood, bearable. Ceremonies for birth and death, for love, for the changing of seasons and the rites of human passage. Ceremonies for the vision of the new world and for dealing with evil, and for the great mysteries of creation, self-sacrifice, suffering, faith and resurrection. The ceremonies which have made truth bearable for the Jews, for instance, are incredibly powerful – powerful enough to sustain them through exile, exodus, dispersion and holocaust. A few years ago I spent some time in Japan, a country which is in many ways extremely secular, yet one where the power of ceremony remains paramount, the day-to-day ceremonies of politeness which make the truth of an overcrowded, hierarchical, familial society bearable, the ancient ceremonies for everything from drinking tea and preparing raw fish to the honouring of the graves of the ancestors, which, though they may actually be performed by few people, nevertheless for millions more, define what it is to be Japanese.

The power of ceremony is twofold. It allows us as individuals to relate to our own lives in a way which takes us beyond meaningless-ness and despair, a way which allows us to pose a question, and, if not an answer, a resolution. And this in forms and modes which draw on all the creativity of the human spirit, in art and music and drama, in architecture and the work of our hands, in words and movement and silence; and in the use of all the symbols which have ancient and ever-new power – light and darkness, colour, procession, withdrawal and the ordinary things of life – the table and the basin, the bread and the wine. All this to express something that is not different or detached from everyday life, but which transfigures it with significance and meaning. The most powerful ceremonies, the ones which sustain us through life and death, are the ones in which all have a part to play, however small.

And, secondly, ceremony has the power to unify, to create community. A common experience on its own will not do that. We share many common experiences, but they do not make us into a community. What unifies us is the naming and symbolizing of the common experience, and we do that first and foremost through ceremony. George MacLeod, the founder of the Iona Community, said, 'Only a demanding common task builds community.' The Iona Community was founded to be a sign of the rebuilding of the common life, the reintegration of the sacred and the secular, of prayer and politics, of the material and the spiritual. The common task through which it set about this rebuilding was the restoration of the ruined monastic buildings on the island of Iona. But the ceremony which named this common task took place every morning before the day's labours began.

In the Abbey church, ministers and craftsmen stood to make their responses:

Unless the Lord builds the house
They labour in vain that build it.

Unless the Lord keeps the city
The watchman waketh but in vain.

O Lord, do good in thy good pleasure
Build thou the walls of Jerusalem.

O God, make speed to save us
O Lord, make haste to help us.

Praise ye the Lord
The Lord's name be praised.

And so, in the words of the Hundred and Twenty-Seventh Psalm, the Community named the truth that defined the common task. And the Abbey was rebuilt, and the Community was built. Without that ceremony to remind us of that truth, it would not have happened. The two are inseparable.

The building of community is crucial to human existence, for only in community can justice and love be done. Only in community is found responsibility – the activity of responding, the demands of accountability to and for others. This, St Paul tells us, is the nature of the church – to be the Body, wherein no part acts independently of another, and wherein if one part hurts, all are hurt, wherein we are interdependent.

The failure of the church

It is not that people have become so materially minded that they are dead to the life of the spirit. My belief is rather that a vast number of people have failed to find, in the church, ceremonies which vividly, meaningfully and with integrity express the truths which they struggle to bear. It is not our message which is at fault. I believe that Christian message to be one which most profoundly addresses, cares for and gives hope to the human condition, and Jesus Christ to be the person who most perfectly integrates the material and the spiritual, human and divine totally at one, and with the transcendent power that such a unity bestows. Not the message, nor any real or imagined predisposition on the part of the hearers. The problem lies in the naming of the truth and, from that, the failure to define the demanding common task.

So, where have we gone wrong? I want to refute this notion that what I am concerned with is merely ritual or practice or form without content. Ceremony is not just about worship, and where it is about worship, it is not merely a question of a particular style of worship. But ceremony is something that surrounds almost everything we do, not only the explicitly religious, but also the apparently secular. Almost every job has its own ceremony, whether it be the office party, the miners' gala, or the nineteenth hole at the golf club. Education and recreation have their ceremonies too, their rituals and symbols. The exclusively male world has ceremony to unify. And the exclusively female world also has its ceremonies, though they may be less formal. Even personal relationships are bound around by ceremony. When people are deprived of meaningful ceremonies, they will discover others, which may be more trivial, less satisfying, less comprehensive. It may be that the seeds of the present frenzied Christmas extravaganza, which is so abhorrent to so many Christians, were sown in the not-too-distant past, when people's need for ceremony was denied to all but the most austere intellectual understanding. For always, when the need for ceremony is denied, there will be people who, for a price, will step in and give people a substitute, which may well, as in the case of Christmas, be tawdry and third-rate. The advertising industry knows well that the power of Christmas ceremony is very strong, and touches on something deeply rooted in the heart.

There have been times when all the events described above were expressed in ceremony that incorporated an overtly Christian understanding of the truth therein. Times when ceremony expressed the belief in the dignity of all work, including and especially manual work, and in the unique value of each individual regardless of occupation. Times when education was celebrated as the ability to create the enquiring spirit, not the production of people conditioned to narrow vision in one field. Times when the ceremonies of recreation allowed the enjoyment of the communal, and were not reduced to talking heads on a screen or a voice in the ears shutting out all real human noise.

We have too easily given up our truth. Or handed it over to others to express, for the truth still continues to find expression – it will out. And especially, we have done it in worship.

We have a service every Tuesday night in the Abbey on Iona, in which we pray by name for people who are sick, and lay hands on any who wishes to receive this ministry. Over many years of participating in this service, I have been forced to ask questions, and to draw some conclusions. By far the largest number who come to receive the laying on of hands are people who fall into a category which might be broadly termed those in search of spiritual healing. But even then, there are many people who come forward who I know are not troubled in their faith, who are not despondent and cast down beyond what is usual, who are not in mourning or addicts or whatever. People go forward to receive the laying on of hands to be healed of anger, of greed, of fear, of selfishness and of all the other things that make all of us broken people. People in large numbers, perhaps sixty or seventy at a time, and many of them young people, receive the laying on of hands because they are seeking absolution. And a ceremony in which we invoke the presence of God's Spirit, and symbolize our care as a church by our touch, makes that absolution real to people. Touch is such a basic human need, and something that is so often alien to our culture, especially for men, that when it is received in a way that is non-threatening, it comes as a real liberation. It is an experience of grace, a moment of making whole. It is, if you like, a sacrament.

But I am glad that, almost accidentally, we have found a ceremony which has real meaning for people in this way. The undeniable and significant need for absolution expressed here has led me to question the way in which we name the most fundamental truth of the Christian church, that of the forgiveness of sins.

In the Church of Scotland, we have no structure for individual confession and absolution. We depend solely on our corporate worship to do this, while giving very little guidance for personal confession. And prayers of confession in church are so often wordy affairs in which the minister repents at length for all his or her sins, or uses the confession as a way to lecture the congregation, that they are inadequate to allow people to unburden their souls in any real way. Or, even if confession is taken seriously, absolution is not. It is so often a formula, which has meaning only for those with a strongly developed intellectual understanding of the forgiveness of sins, and does nothing for those whose apprehension of faith is primarily emotional or intuitive. When we lament the level of commitment that we find in our churches, we would do well to ask ourselves how much we allow the experience of grace a way through our worship, and how much our worship actually gets in the way of that experience. Sometimes it seems that the only conclusion possible is that we do not know ourselves to be a forgiven people. Oh, we may believe it with our minds, but do we know it in our hearts?

Naming our truth

It seems to me that there are a number of ways in which we have failed in our task of naming the truth in ways which have meaning for people. First of all, we simply have not cared enough, have taken too lightly the need to offer people the best that we can. We have failed to offer God the best that we can. We have lost the sense of worship as a drama in which the great salvation story is told – and along with that loss, we have easily used dead language, dead forms, and the power which they had in the past no longer communicates itself today. It is a work of great love and care to discern what of our tradition is appropriate, and what needs to be expressed in new ways. It is a hard work. But it is absolutely crucial. We take far too much for granted.

We too easily forget that the Christian message is to the whole person, and needs to be comprehended thus. The reformed churches have placed great emphasis on the centrality of the word and, as a corrective to forms which ignored our capacity to reason and understand, that was essential. But we do not worship only with our minds. True worship engages the whole person – the emotions, the senses, the will, the intuition, as well as the intellect. I can quite see that the Covenanters worshipping on bare hillsides, with the knowledge of persecution always before them, were wholly engaged. But does our worship do that today?

And, as the message is to the whole person, it is also to the whole community body. Participation is of the essence of meaningful ceremony. But too much of our worship life is non-participatory. I do not just mean the use of responses in worship. That is only one form of participation. There used to be a tradition of people praying aloud in church – I mean the ordinary members of the congregation. How often do we give people the opportunity, the motivation, the confidence, for prepared and extempore prayer? Most people would have a heart attack if you suggested it. We have silenced people in church. And how often do we use the vast resource of experience, gifts with words, insight and commitment that there is in any church? Of course, to do that takes time, training, encouragement, patience. But anyone, no matter how unlikely, can take a part in the leadership of worship. We talk about the priesthood of all believers, but do we mean it?

And then there is the abstraction of worship from everyday life. We pray and preach grandly about abstractions. Where is our faith, that we do not pray and preach enough about the difficulties of bringing up children, or of living on social security, or of being under enormous pressure at work, or about the strains of marriage, or of what it feels like to be labelled because you are a single parent, or a homosexual or disabled? These are what concern people for most of their waking hours, these are the issues that disturb their sleep. But more than that, they are the channels to people's care, the means of raising awareness of the struggles of others, and their own links with these others.

And we have allowed worship to be anaesthetized in the interest of modernity, rationality, being in tune. We have not had the courage of our convictions and have acted as if we too do not believe in the spiritual as a given of life. We have allowed others to do the task that was handed on to us – of investing with meaning and significance every high occasion and every passing moment. Look at what we have done with death! One of the two absolutes of human existence, and we have allowed its occasion to be utterly sanitized. Instead of a ceremony that honours a life, admits a death, confronts reality and calls forth grief and agony and hope from the bereft, people now die in secret, and are despatched from behind death-denying velvet curtains, while mourners are forbidden at all costs from making a scene, from weeping, from being a spectacle. And now psychology is telling us what we knew all along but were too craven to hold on to, that people need to be confronted with the reality of death, need to mourn in order that the healing process may begin.

And, finally, we have allowed our ceremony to become exclusive rather than inclusive. We have used ceremony as many people use it, but the church of all should not, to define some people as outsiders, and ourselves as insiders. This is a very terrible and dangerous thing to do. In the past, it happened through fear and ignorance. So poor and innocent and wise women became witches, were cast in the role of other, and all the superstition of ignorance and the terror of the unknown were projected on to them, and a million of them were done to death. But the message of Jesus is that there is no 'other'. When ceremony becomes exclusive, when it names itself over against the other, instead of being an expression of corporate love, care, awe and hope, it becomes an expression of corporate hate, fear, disgust and despair. And from ceremonies that perverted truth, that were deeply and fundamentally exclusive, all that was humane and sensible in ordinary folk revolted. And still revolts. The ceremonies lose their credibility, and all hope of a credible truth being shared is gone. The only safeguard against the perversion of ceremony is to stand firmly by the comprehensiveness that is expressed so strongly in the Christian message – the love of God for all people at all times, in all places. When we lose this inclusiveness, we lay ourselves open to terrible temptations. The Rev. Greg Dixon, National Secretary until recently for the Moral Majority in the United States of America, urged his followers to pray for the death of their opponents, claiming, 'We are tired of turning the other cheek . . . Good heavens, that's all we have done.' Such false prophets cannot conceive of God as also of the enemy.

Rediscovering ceremonies of life

What can we do? Perhaps we might rediscover ceremony which builds into all human life a naming of the Christian truth. That truth is clearly expressed in the Gospels, and there are intimations there, and in the history of the church, and in the church of the poor today, and in the creativity of Christians everywhere, which might help us.

We might begin to rediscover the ceremony of welcome and hospitality, so important to Jesus, who valued the welcome he received from so many people, in so many homes, and who washed the feet of his friends. There are many ceremonies in our culture around meals, and Jesus constantly used feasts, meals and the table where all were welcome as a sign of the kingdom. We ignore the ceremony of meals at our cost. And how many of us maintain the ceremony of giving thanks for food. Perhaps it is too uncomfortable for us, when we know that others starve while we eat. All the more reason to give thanks, and to remember that to pray 'Give us this day our daily bread' is a prayer of anguish for millions. And the ceremony of blessing. This is a gift we can give one another which has never in my experience been refused, by Christian and non-Christian alike.

The ceremony of sanctuary is one which is being wonderfully rediscovered by the church in North America, offering refuge to refugees fleeing repression in Central America, and thank God for it. But what about our churches? Have we created alternative forms of sanctuary to serve when all our churches are always shut? And the ceremonies of celebration, of the marking of important occasions? They don't have to be boozy, maudlin events full of pathos, or stuffy formal occasions. Or what about the ceremonies of the family? They are among the most powerful of all, and they will arise anyway, so we can choose to be intentional about them. My children love sharing in communion round a meal table. Then it becomes something which includes them, something which they can understand.

Or the ceremonies of solidarity with the poor and the oppressed? Or birth and marriage and death? I believe that one of the reasons that there has been such a strong reaction against modern maternity practice is not just about the right to choose how to have a baby. It is also that huge hospitals, with all the paraphernalia of high technology, do not make it easy to have appropriate ceremonies for something as important as birth. It is hard to experience fully the uniqueness of birth when one feels like the next one on the production line.

And, finally, I want to say that we must never underestimate the power, or fail to guard it, of the central ceremonies of the Christian church. Both baptism and communion have a way of naming the essential truths of Christianity in ways which are unsurpassed. Water, bread and wine – there are no more powerful symbols, and they represent no more powerful truths. Let us take care how we use them. Let us ask questions of what it says to people to see communion as a black-coated and severe proceeding, served out in little glasses and neatly diced cubes of bread. Let us ask what it says to people to see it as something that can be administered only by men. These ceremonies have meaning and power for us, and part of that is the meaning and power of the familiar. But in the way we carry them out, are we sure that they are faithful to the truth they are naming?

If there is a special calling to some in the church, a special task to which some are ordained and set apart, it is, I believe, not primarily a pastoral one, nor a preaching one, nor even a sacramental one. It is a task which includes all of these, although not as the exclusive possession of the ordained. It is rather to take, as calling and charge, the responsibility of ensuring that the spiritual in human existence and the material in human existence are not tangential but integral. It is to cherish and nurture the truth that God is for all of life, and in all of life. It is to be dedicated to ensuring that the ceremony which people so desperately seek and need to make truth bearable, both in the expression of the individual spirit and in the creating of the community of justice and love, is given worthy expression, and truly, clearly and joyfully names the truth in which we trust, that of the Word made flesh.

Coracle, *Winter 1991.*

20
The Heavens Declare the Glory of God

In the old days in Scotland, every child was expected to know the Shorter Catechism off by heart, and every child could answer the question 'What is man's chief end?' with the words 'Man's chief end is to glorify God'.

To glorify God. Glory is a very old word, whose meaning is sometimes hard to uncover. It seems an imprecise word conveying many shades of meaning; awesome, mysterious, uncomfortable sometimes. And yet, there is the huge sense of beauty and power underlying that.

In Hebrew, the word that is translated by 'glory' is the word *Kabod*, which means literally the weight or value of something. And so, in a religious context it has come to mean the worth or value of God, what we see and appreciate shining out from the mystery that we call God. To see the glory of God is to appreciate the value of God.

The glory of God has inspired countless generations of poets and artists and musicians who have struggled to express the inexpressible, that which cannot be explained or contained within philosophy or discursive prose. It needs a heart language to begin to pour out an overflowing of dread and delight. We sing when we cannot speak. Most of us have forgotten how to dance, if indeed, we ever knew, but people, including King David, danced their ecstasy.

And it is perhaps the impulse to glorify that flings us face down on the grass to smell the earth, or sends a shiver through us as we watch waves crashing in on a shoreline and imaginatively ride the rolling seas. Nowhere is it easier to see the glory of God than in the glory of creation. It would take a hardened heart indeed, or, rather, seriously dulled senses, to fail to be moved by the grandeur of mountains or the tenacious fragility of the primrose in spring, by the changing moods of the sky and the turbulent, charged air. This week, blessed by sunshine and rain, we have had many chances to delight in the glory of creation.

And yet, as well as in the beauty, there is glory also in the absurdity of creation. The thistle. as much as the rose, the crow as much as the blackbird, the slug as much as the butterfly, are written into the music of creation. They are part of the same concert. The word 'concert' means literally, struggling together, and the divine music holds within it, formed into the most delicate and carefully harmonized score, many dissonances.

And so it is with the glory of God expressed in human creation. It is not only in the ardent lover, the faithful friend, the wise counsellor, the trusting child that we see God's glory. There is glory also in the anger of the oppressed, the pain of the wounded, the loneliness of the despised. It is the glory of God that puts such as these first in the kingdom of heaven, and makes us all interdependent – as much a part of the delicate and complex structure of relationship as the plants and animals that need the trees of the forest to survive.

We are all part of God's creation – created, redeemed and liberated by the love of God, shown so vividly in Jesus. *We* are God's glory, and to glorify God we need to recognize that glory in others, and tend it. 'The glory of God is a human being fully alive.' So said Irenaeus, and so we might remember. We can see the value of care for God's creation in nature – the need to protect and conserve and renew. The same care is required of us for the human creation, to appreciate what God has given, and goes on giving. We glorify God not just with our words and feelings, but with our actions, with our whole lives. When, as Paul says, we are able to live a way that is in harmony with God, then we glorify God.

God is glorified, not just in the passionate phrases of the poet, the bold strokes of the artist, the beauty of the choir and the graceful movements of the dancer. God is also glorified in the anger of those who cannot stand by and see God's image tarnished in the fellow human being by injustice, poverty, war and cruelty. God is glorified in the endurance of all those who go on

daring to live whilst labouring under the burdens of unemployment, homelessness, squalor and misery. God is glorified in the
struggling together of everyone who strives against all the odds
and all the evidence to demonstrate that human beings can live
together in peace. God is glorified in the quiet movements of all
those who care for the very old, the sick, for children, and in
those who have absolutely nothing to give but themselves, aware
of weakness and fallibility, and give them anyway.

Our chief end is to glorify God – not to crawl on the altar of a
vain and jealous God who wants us to be fearful and obsequious,
but to admire and appreciate beyond words the love of a God
who wants to share a good thing with us. Alice Walker, in her
classic *The Color Purple* writes: 'People think pleasing God is
all God cares about. But any fool living in the world can see God
is always trying to please us back.' Glorifying God in the poetry
of compassion, in the tasks of faithfulness, in the concert of
unity, and in the dance of creation. This is our chief end. This is
what we were made to do.

Iona Abbey, May 1987.

PART THREE

Through the Year

21
Living in the Cracks

First Sunday in Advent
Isaiah 52.1–10; 1 Thessalonians 5.1–11; Luke 21.25–33

A friend of mine wrote recently: *all theology is, in the end, biography.* I think what he meant is that in the Bible, and in the history of the church, we find the story of how human beings in different times and places experienced God acting in their lives, as individuals, as communities and as nations. The Bible tells the stories of men and women and children, and of how their encounter with God changed them, shook them up, set them travelling in new directions, often where they did not expect or even want to go. All of these stories are old, some of them thousands of years old, and yet all of them have a relevance and freshness still. Because, although they recount what happened to people in very different cultures, places and times, and although they may have related to experiences which we have not had, nevertheless, through the lives of these distant but very human men and women, they illustrate realities of life which are constant. The great mysteries of birth and death, of suffering and celebration, of justice and freedom, of loss and discovery and demand, are every bit as real as they ever were, and people still struggle to make sense of these mysteries, still ask questions of meaning and value about work and money, about love and hate, about how to care for our children and how to live in harmony with our neighbours.

So I don't find it hard to discover myself in these three very diverse, dark and somewhat apocalyptic readings we heard from the Bible today, readings which are traditional for the beginning of the time of preparation we call Advent. Let's look at the three very different situations, divided by centuries, not only from our time but from each other.

The passage from Isaiah comes from a time in the eighth century BC when many of the people of Israel were in exile in Babylon, crushed and without hope. They were what we would call euphemistically today 'guest workers', with few rights, struggling in an alien, unfriendly and dominant culture to hang on to their identity which was summed up in their religion. And unlike the exile in Egypt, this time they had been forced into captivity far from their beloved land, divided from their fellow Israelites lamenting their exile at home, but militarily and politically powerless to do anything about it. Well, we are not unfamiliar in the twentieth century with any of these things – with guest workers, with forced captivity, with a people divided, with a people struggling to retain their identity in the face of adversity. On *this* day, somewhere in the world, all of these things are happening.

And the second passage comes from one of Paul's letters to the church in Thessalonica, an important city of the Roman Empire in what is present-day Greece. In this, Paul is writing to a small community of faith, practising a minority religion in the face of resentment and opposition from the established religion. Again, not an unfamiliar situation, one we can possibly sympathize with. Both the shock and the appeal of the new have always attracted fierce hostility. On *this* day, somewhere in the world, these things are happening.

And the gospel passage is that disturbing one from Luke's Gospel in which Jesus interprets the strange things happening on the earth, and gives a warning note to his followers. In the gospel narratives, this incident happens very near to the time of Jesus' death, just before he ate the passover meal with his friends in the upper room. Here is a place buzzing with rumours, following a hero's welcome in the city; here is a religious and political establishment threatened by the subversive teachings of this strange man, who was so popular with the ordinary people, and determined to get rid of him for fear he might challenge their power base. And here is a man, facing imminent arrest and death, knowing that he was approaching the time of his ultimate testing, not knowing whom to trust, unsure even of his closest followers.

No wonder the mood was dark and apocalyptic. We know that Jesus himself believed that the end time was very close, the Day of the Lord, and that he expected it to come during the lifetime of his hearers. Even he still had to discover the depth of the mystery of God's ways. But leaving that aside, this was a time of extremity – of the closeness of death and the whisper of treason, of a religious and social revolution, of a paradigm shift in the understanding of God. In such times, natural and human phenomena take on an extra significance; there is a heightening of tension, a sense of being very close to the edge.

I think it is not fanciful to detect some of this same heightening of tension in our own society. The increase in many kinds of violence: the violence of terrorism, the violence of assault, the violence of poverty, the violence of redundancy with no prospect even of the kind of steady manual labour which gave so many in the past the dignity of work; the shock of technology with its promises and dangers; the violence of the media, whether in violent language and images and the violation of personhood, or in the violence of pornography, or in the violence of interactive video games; the violence of assaults at every level, from the street to the Houses of Parliament, on the weakest and most vulnerable, all constitute a culture of violence, finding its apotheosis in the terrible killing of a child by children. And the cracking and crumbling of many of the building blocks of our culture – the expectations that show little prospect of being fulfilled, the certainties that have turned into huge question marks, the security that now seems anything but safe, the old verities found wanting. And all this in the context of seemingly ineradicable famine in Africa, the hell of Bosnia, wars and rumours of war, and destruction everywhere, environmental degradation, and the fear that accompanies AIDS, which illness is being remembered worldwide today. When the building blocks crumble, people have to learn to live in the cracks, and there are many ways of living there between the no-longer and the not-yet, in the shadow of the falling masonry.

People have always struggled with achieving a healthy and happy balance between individual freedom and community responsibility. Take away the intrinsic worth and dignity, their freedom to be subject, not object, reduce them to cogs in a machine or functionaries in a state apparatus, and you end up with something like the Pandora's box of former Yugoslavia – when the lid blows off, so much of value is destroyed in the explosion. Break the relationship between the individual and his or her environment, natural and social, and people lose a sense of commitment and corporate responsibility for one another. It becomes dog eat dog, and the survival of the strongest and the most ruthless.

And all the situations of our three passages were also struggling with this tension, not least Jesus in Jerusalem. Cause and effect, action and reaction, the swing of the pendulum, and people get caught in the middle, foundering, dodging missiles, looking for new blueprints. Without a personal framework and infrastructure of discipline and patience that comes from involvement in caring relationships with others, whether that be friends, a family, a community, a nation, then our liberty becomes a miserable and self-defeating licence which is very far from liberating. Without the love and encouragement that values the unique and distinctive persons we have the capacity to be, locked into a straitjacket that demands conformity and stunts the spirit, then our discipline becomes brutal and unforgiving. And the abuse of power feeds on both these polarized positions.

So, from inside our crack, in our time of extremity, what is the word mediated to us through the prophet, the apostle and the Lord, which makes these readings our story as well? I think we can discern three notes, three refrains running through all of these passages.

The first is a word of hope. Without hope, people die. Without the hope that things can change, there is little incentive for anything. Without hope, it is hard for people to love, and if we cannot love, we cannot will change, we cannot be disciples, learners, those who struggle with patience and endurance to bring the future into being. Without hope, we have no investment in the future and, therefore, no investment in the present. But Isaiah speaks of a liberation from captivity, of peace and homecoming and the restoration of joy. It is an encouraging, inspiring message for a people near despair. And Paul, striking a graver note, reminds the Thessalonians of the grace of God, that great glowing passion of his, the grace of light and enlightenment and the forbearance of anger. And Jesus, the most sombre of all, yet sees in the signs and portents the fact that salvation, real liberation, is near. In all of these, utterly present to the speakers, is the power of God to bring hope out of despair, to bring the new into being, to confound the dreary cycles of cause and effect, to make of the cracks, of the black earth of death, the seedbed of resurrection. So the first word is hope, and we who follow Jesus must nurture and cherish and embody our hope, not as an easy optimism, nor as an easy answer, but as a way and in a way.

And the second word is one of warning. A warning that the fearful, the unexpected, the threatening, will happen. A warning against thinking you can predict how or what it will be. A warning against thinking, *this means someone else* or *I'm all right, I'm safe*. The warning is that the only real security is in the hope and in the way. This is a *'put not your trust in princes'* word – or in parties, policies, possessions, or even your own purity. It is a word that cautions humility. There can be few of us who have not at some time been the proud, self-congratulatory Pharisee, convinced of our own goodness and the badness of others, pleased at our good fortune and secretly sure that we did it all by ourselves, only to have our little house of cards come crashing down about our ears. This word fatally undermines that position, as so many in the Bible do.

And the third word is one of preparation. Learn to read the signs of the times. Practise discernment. Seek to understand complexity. Be ready; don't be taken by surprise, as by a thief in the night. Like a pregnant woman who does not know when her labour will begin, we can still prepare for the tasks ahead of us. It is a bit like saying, go to your ante-natal classes so that you can co-operate fully and with courage in the birthing process you are engaged in, painful though it will be.

Advent, along with Lent, is a time of preparation. During Lent, we accompany Jesus into the desert; we face the wilderness of our own inner landscape to prepare ourselves for the Easter journey of death and resurrection. During Advent, we go with John into the wilderness to prepare the way to welcome Christ into our hearts and lives anew at Christmas. We have the opportunity to explore the inner geography of our lives for areas of dead wood, thorns or tangled knots. Twisted relationships, the dead wood of old hurts or habits, the confusion that sometimes comes when we feel we can't see the wood for the trees – all these are wilderness areas, and they need to be cleared away before growth and new life is possible. Or perhaps there are desert patches – arid, dry areas where nothing can grow or blossom, parts of us which have almost withered away from not being used or tended or tested – some tenderness, some care, some talent, some forgiveness, some humour – that need the water of life to bring them bursting into flower.

If we have desert or wilderness places within us – and which of us do not? – Advent is a good time to prepare for new life, for the birth of Christ within us, to clear the way so that we have more courageous self-examination, more open hearts, more receptive spirits, more loving kindness towards ourselves and others. We don't and can't know what that will mean for us, and it will probably not be what we expect, but when that call to worship, to accept, and to walk the road of love comes again with renewed vigour, we want to be prepared, to be ready.

So, a word of preparation, sometimes dramatic, sometimes quiet and steady. And the first necessity for our walking the way of love is that we should be on our feet. '*Rise from the dust, undo the chains that bind you*', says Isaiah. '*Be awake and sober*', says Paul. '*Stand up and raise your heads*', says Jesus. We can't walk sitting down, far less crumpled in a heap. To stand up very often means to stand out, and to stand up for the way of love is not, it seems, a very acceptable stance at the moment. Nevertheless, by grace it is both our calling and our charism, our gift, our freedom. Let us encourage and support one another to embrace our calling and our freedom this Advent.

Augustine-Bristo Church, Edinburgh, 1993.

22
Pull Back the Curtain on Bethlehem's Stable

Third Sunday in Advent

Ask any number of women, or men who are much involved in preparation too, what they feel about Christmas, and an awful lot of them will tell you that they hate it, and wish someone would do away with it. The way we celebrate Christmas , especially for those with large families, is a huge amount of work – cards to write, presents to buy and wrap, parties to organize and attend, and a dinner to make which is infinitely more complicated than the usual. Decorations to hang, a tree to put up – the list is seemingly endless. Magazines and newspapers are full of Christmas advice – recipes, ideas for gifts, new ways with tinsel – all the way through to plans for managing Christmas without tears; huge lists of times and dates that start back in November, and run with a military precision that suggests something more like the Normandy landings than a time of celebration. And the final insult is the pages in the Sunday supplements of the year's best books – just in case you find time hanging on your hands, presumably.

And it's not just at home that there's more work. Thousands of people work long hours of overtime through December, in shops and restaurants especially. And all this in the context of arguments, fighting with Christmas crowds and traffic, embarrassed conversations about where Aunt Mary will spend Christmas, and the real pain of those who, because they are alone, or their family situation doesn't measure up to the Christmas-card ideal, or they're mourning, feel that in some way they are failures. And the agonizing pressures, especially if we have children, to spend more than we can afford, to the extent of going seriously into debt. You only have to listen to our conversations to realize that the great British Christmas resembles nothing so much as a military campaign, at the end of which people sit down to their Christmas dinner exhausted, emotionally worn-out, and in greater danger of suicide, or marital or mental breakdown than at any other time of the year. The other kind of Christmas article in magazines recognizes this: they're full of advice about how to get away from Christmas; a week in the Bahamas if you have the money, a good book and a bottle of whisky if you don't, and a sign on the door that says *Do not disturb.*

Why do we do it? Why do we go on putting ourselves through this punishment? Cynics would say it's all the result of crass commercialism, that we are the victims of exploitation in a con- sumer society, fallen prey to the greatest marketing opportunity of them all. Religious cynics would say that Christmas is more about the worship of mammon than God, more about glory to the High Street than glory to God in the highest.

But I don't believe that. I don't know *anyone* who actually likes the crass commercialization of Christmas, and I know a great many people who, even if they are not religious, try very hard to make it a more appropriate festival. For most of us, Christmas is something we try to keep *in spite of*, rather than because of advertising and commercialism, and we fight to get through the glitter and the mire to the important things at the heart of Christmas.

And what are these important things? I believe that Christmas matters very much, even to people who are not Christian, because it takes account of some very basic human needs.

There is the need to make the effort, even once a year, to keep in touch with friends, to let them know they're not forgotten. There is the need, even once in a year, to try and pick up the threads of broken relationships, to mend what has been torn, to weave these threads back into the fabric of our lives. Christmas gives people that chance, that excuse, we might say. And though the effort is often doomed to failure, partly because it's hard not to be over-optimistic in our expectations, there's nothing wrong with the intention.

There's the age-old need of people to have a festival, especially in the depths of winter, to break the long, dark nights and the grey and dreary days with a little colour and magic, to anticipate the coming of the light. And the age-old need of people simply to celebrate, to have days that are different, to affirm the human spirit. Even the poorest people, perhaps especially the poorest people, need to have the possibility of extravagance, of knowing they are worth more than just their labour, worth more than the unrelieved anxiety of their days. There are Christmas preparations going on even in Cardboard City. People need times when they can put down the burden of daily living and say, today we will be happy, today we will simply appreciate.

And all of us in our war-torn world yearn for something that will give us hope and the vision of a better world. We know that this Christmas people will still kill one another in the name of something or other. This Christmas, people will still starve to death in a world of food mountains. This Christmas, our country will still be on the easy road to individualism and the crueller manifestations of the law, and away from community. This Christmas, the same people we pray for today will still be, many of them, hurt, bewildered, weary or unendurably lonely. It is, in part, this yearning for hope, this longing for a better world, that makes people who otherwise have no faith connection, fill churches on Christmas Eve, listen to carols, and hear and ache for this magic of shepherds and angels, of starlight on a cold mountain, of a stable and a baby, of peace on earth and goodwill to all. *'Behold, I tell you a mystery'* is still a powerful message.

But most of all, Christmas is for the children. We do it for the children. I don't just mean our own children; I mean all our children. We do it for the next generation, for the future. We recognize that there is an enormous security in the Christmas story, even for those who are not Christian. Christmas seems like a respite from fear, a time out from the dreads and insecurities that make us so afraid. This beautiful and intimate story of love and birth and mystery has the power to touch even hardened hearts. We want to pass that security on to our children, the security that is symbolized by trees and lights and carols and presents; we go to extraordinary lengths to give our children these things.

But it's not really just the children around us, is it? We do it also for the child in us. Some of the reassuring power of Christmas is rooted in our own childhoods – in that far-off time when things were familiar and safe and predictable, when we were not burdened with the cares and disappointments of adulthood, when we had no need to be afraid for our children, for our friends, for the world. In *a time of innocence, a time of confidences* (Paul Simon). And even if our childhoods were not like that, it's the way we would like them to have been. When we say *Christmas is a time for the children*, perhaps deep down we are saying, *Christmas is a time when we can once again relive our ideal childhood and not be afraid.*

Nostalgia, the security of childhood, the joys of festivity, the warmth of friendship. These are good and kind things, part of the spirit of Christmas. But they are not enough, and this is the point at which those who approach Christmas from a purely human perspective can go no farther. These things, good as they are, are inadequate to release us from the bondage of fear. They will not do for the nights of despair when we lie sleepless, questioning everything we have been taught to hold dear. They will not do for the rushes of panic which sweep over us when we visualize ourselves or our children lost, hurting, in torment. They will not do when we weep for the earth, for its poisoned rivers and polluted air and devastated life systems, nor when we cry in sympathy with the mother who has seen her child shot in crossfire, or with a father whose little girl has been raped and murdered. They will not do for the fear that has caused millions of people across the world to make great waves of human migration, or build prisons to stifle dissent. They will not do for the knock on the door in the middle of the night, or the fear of holocaust, or the word of finality from the doctor. And even those of us who generally live in peace and contentment, even for us, fear is always round the corner; fear of failure, fear of loneliness, fear of sickness and death. The fear that lies deep within us is powerful, paralysing, threatening. Such a fear demands more than the joys of human community, the comforts of nostalgia, the healing effects of beauty summed up, even in one of the most delight-full stories ever told.

I would dearly love to be able to approach the coming Christmas with the delight and awe of the children. Perhaps only they can fully enter into the kingdom of the Christ-child. But I am not a child. I am not innocent. I have eaten of the fruits of the tree of knowledge of good and evil, and what I know of myself, and of the world, taints my delight. 'When I was a child,' says Paul, 'I thought as a child, but now that I am a man, I have put away childish things.' There is no going back to innocence.

And I have found, in what seems like a reversal, but is perhaps true for more people than admit it, that I find great joy in Easter and great pain in Christmas. If all we have to hold on to as a sign of hope is birth and innocence and looking back, then we are above all people to be pitied. If the cradle of Christmas is a sign of the birth of love, then the cross and empty tomb are the signs of love crucified and yet rising triumphantly in new birth and new life. Our experience of life is that so much that is good and beautiful and hopeful becomes corrupted by our capacity to choose, often without intending or even knowing it, what is bad and life-denying. So much turns sour. But the resurrection of Easter has the power to restore in us a kind of new innocence, a being born again, a re-naissance, which lets us be touched and moved by the mystery of Christmas.

If we are to be able to sing the Gloria with the angels – Glory to God in the highest, and on earth peace – and have it really mean something more than pretty tunes, then we have to know that it is good news we hear, the great glad tidings that have the power to transform our lives and enable us to live, not free from fear, because we shall always have fearful times, but free of being controlled by our fear, and able to find new hope out of our suffering. That is good news that goes all the way to Easter and beyond. It is the news that says to us first of all that we are loved – without condition, without limit, beyond measure. At Christmas, the word made flesh in Jesus says 'I am for you'. Our lives are precious to God.

But that is not all. Not only are we loved. The good news of Christmas is that we *can* love. We know that we are far from perfect, that failure is an experience common to us all. But by grace, we are not defined by our failure. We still have space to grow in love. This is the meaning of forgiveness – our existential reality – that we are forgiven people, and that we can forgive. And as we grow in love, we will grow in courage too. Only trusting in love, in our forgivenness, in the knowledge that we are not defined by our failures, gives us courage enough to face our fears and feel our fears and know that we will come out the other side. That love is the light that shines in the darkness and will never be put out, even when we don't see anything but black. That love is eternal, and endures when all else is lost. That love replaces our childish clinging to security with a childlike trust and spontaneity.

This good news – that we are loved, that we can love – needs one thing more to make Christmas really real. It needs to be shared. Not hugged to ourselves, like a private affair, not even kept within the safety of church walls. It needs to be told out, not in words but in action. The word became flesh, not more words. It lived among us. We give glory to God by *living* good news, by being the word of love become flesh; in our healing of wounds, in our restoring of right relationships, in our struggle for justice, in our daily care-giving, in our delight in life.

Christmas and Easter are one. Without an Easter faith, our Christmas celebrations are childish and partial, and, in the end, not so much frivolous as tragic. With an Easter faith, Christmas is a means to discover the absolutely precious gift at the centre.

Pull back the curtain on Bethlehem's stable
Strip off the tinsel and peer through the dark,
Look at the child who's a threat, yet in danger,
Homeless and helpless, he first makes his mark.
Love's the secret, love's the secret
Love is God's cradle, God's table, God's cup and God's ark.

(John L. Bell)

Lansdowne Church, Glasgow, 1990.

23
No Glass Cases

The Naming of Jesus

This child is chosen by God for the destruction and
salvation of many in Israel. He will be a sign from God which
many people will speak against, and so reveal their secret
thoughts. And sorrow, like a sharp sword, will break
your own heart.

(Luke 2.34–5, GNB)

The end of one year and the beginning of a new one is always the
occasion for much reflection and review, personally and in the
media, as we stand two-faced, like a Greek mask, looking both
back and forwards. This year there seems to be even more of it
about, and the general consensus is that 1992 was a very bad
year, one which most people are glad to see the back of. It's
not hard to see why – war and famine, destruction and racism,
disease and drought stalk the world abroad, while at home,
homelessness and unemployment, recession and the dreary
manoeuvres of a country governed by economic not political values make grounds for optimism hard to find. Environmentalists
tell us that the planet cannot afford economic growth; politicians
tell us that people can't not afford it; at the Earth Summit in Rio
these two positions clashed and nobody won.

On a smaller level, 1992 was not a very enlightening year
either. As people in high places displayed little integrity, more
and more ordinary people discovered themselves, their jobs and
their communities to be expendable, and the media found ever-
new ways to sell papers by wading in mud and misery and being
insufferably morally superior about it.

Cynics, and not just cynics, might say that it's all a sign of the decline of a dominant Western culture which has no values other than those of the marketplace. Religious people might lament the drop in churchgoing as a reason for decaying moral standards; non-religious people might point to the horrors of religious bigotry as evidence that superstition and not reason still rules. Often we find ourselves caught in the tension of feeling deeply unhappy about what is going on around us, but not knowing how to challenge the huge impersonal forces that swirl us and our world about.

I imagine that Mary and Joseph may have felt much the same – living in an occupied country, trekking around it to register for a census, feeling nervous and uncertain about their somewhat unconventional marital relationship, and above all, caught up in events over which they had very little control.

In the midst of the gloom and ugliness of the world at present, we peer through the tinsel and tawdriness of so much of our commercial Christmas as if to find the precious jewel at the centre – the Nativity, that birth, that magical story of mystery and starlight and angels singing that glows through time and space to lighten our darkness, to warm our hearts, to dazzle our senses. And so we should, because it is indeed infinitely precious, that moment of love and self-sacrifice and cherishing, that moment of freely-chosen obedience and risk and hope, that moment of God speaking.

But we should not forget that the precious jewel of the incarnation does not sit outside history like a gem in a glass case, or a scene in one of these paperweights that children shake. The birth of Jesus was also set in the midst of gloom and ugliness, of corruption and power-politics. And Mary and Joseph, just as we do, had to struggle with the interface between personal hopes and political struggles.

In the Christmas narratives, we can see a curious thing. We can see just how much is happening, how much is going on round this insignificant Jewish couple and their tiny baby, not just in the birth but in its aftermath. Strange visitors, bearing gifts, right enough, even if somewhat unsuitable for a baby, but well-intentioned. But the end of *that* story was something different: a brutal military repression, set in motion unintentionally by the foreigners whose well-meaning arrival in the wrong place aroused suspicions and created new dangers. And so the travellers from the East are suddenly seen in a new light.

> We call them wise
> And I had always thought of them that way
> respecting the pilgrimage of anyone
> who sees a star and follows it
> to his discomforting –
> being prepared to change.
> And yet –
> in following their star, the star
> that was to lead them to
> enlargement of the soul (their own) . . .
> they blundered mightily, and set in train
> the massacre of many innocents.
> Naive and foolish men they were, not wise,
> to go and ask of Herod 'Where's
> your rival, where
> is he who might unseat you?'
>
> I wonder if, back
> in their own countries,
> for all that they themselves were born again,
> they heard the voice of Rachel
> weeping for her children
> refusing to be comforted
> because they were no more?
> (Kate Compston – *Bread of Tomorrow*)

And the final result of that well-intentioned visit – flight into Egypt, refugees fleeing in fear, political forces interfering with the personal hopes of one family.

These personal hopes are well described in the second chapter of Luke's Gospel. This very Jewish family did what all devout Jews did at the birth of their first-born son; they named him and took him to the temple in Jerusalem to be dedicated.

Of course, he was named according to the instructions of an angel, which is perhaps a little unusual. But then, children often get their names in unusual ways. I was speaking to Susan Turner, who is our musician this morning, and she was telling me that her little daughter has the name of a medieval Northumbrian monk. Four days before the baby was born, Susan was reading a book in which he was mentioned, and she and her husband decided that it would be a beautiful name for their child. And it is a beautiful name.

But a name is a deeply personal thing. It locates us in our family, our community, our culture, our time, and yet it is uniquely our own. In many cultures, to know someone's name is to have power over them. And a dedication is also a personal event – a statement about our beliefs, our values, our vows and our intentions. And yet, here again, in this absolutely conventional act, the unconventional happens. Two old people recognize the political nature of this child's birth. Simeon speaks words which are both hope and challenge to a whole people, and which also suggest a significance beyond the Jews to the other peoples of the world. And Anna goes to tell the news of the baby to all those in Jerusalem who were waiting for it to be set free from the Roman occupation.

What mixed feelings Mary and Joseph must have had at all this. And how did Mary respond to Simeon's words to her? One might feel, albeit nervously, proud that a child was to bring salvation. But destruction? And the sorrow that was to break her heart? Well, perhaps she was a woman (and perhaps hers was a time) for whom life in all its fullness encompassed times of sorrow and emptiness and grief, more than our relentlessly fearful society with its addictive cravings does.

What these stories reveal to us, however, is that it is not in spite of the fallible and corruptible political events of the world that God acts, but through them, not by denying them but by transforming them. *And* that the incarnation, the Word made flesh, is not a political programme or a religious doctrine or a church law, but a way, a pattern, a stance, a decision. *And* that it is in that very difficult place where the personal meets the political, where *our* needs and hopes encounter the needs and hopes of our fellow men and women, that we walk the Way, give flesh to the Word, have the opportunity to do what the angels cannot do – change a world of hurt and shame into a world of justice, love and peace. At every moment, Christ seeks to be born in us, just as at every moment Christ brings us to die, and to rise to new life.

So if we find ourselves living with tensions, conflicts, the gap between the way life is and the way we hope it could be, then perhaps, like Mary and Joseph, we are blessed, we are in the right place. Because there is the place where following the way of Jesus, the way of practical, down-to-earth love, makes a difference. It is in struggling to discover how to love, how to care, how to do justice, how to be transmitters of new life that we walk with Jesus, not in avoiding that struggle.

And in so doing, we have to learn to let go of worrying about all the things we can't control, and, as Mary did, live and act out of our own obedience and trust. That also means letting go of the need to impose outcomes on ourselves and others, and living by a way. This is not an easy thing to do in a world which has exalted the doctrine of the end justifying the means to an idolatrous status.

But it is my source of hope at the beginning of this year in which there seems little reason for optimism. Because the hope of Jesus goes beyond optimism into a divine reality in which the means of love are never lost or wasted, and cannot finally be overcome. We cannot choose outcomes – but we can choose ways, here and now, day by day, and give birth again and again to the Word made flesh in us.

In the name of God who is mystery, God who is love, God who is freedom. Amen.

Lansdowne Church, Glasgow, 1993.

24
The Love of a Fool

Low Sunday

If you had just initiated an important new venture, and you knew that you had to go away, what kind of person would you look for to take over from you? To whom would you give this very special task?

Would you give it to someone who had consistently let you down over a considerable length of time, who had proved himself to be utterly unreliable not only in times of major crisis, but also in his inability to deliver even the smallest promises he made? Would you give it to someone who could be remarkably obtuse in his grasp of events, who sometimes seemed to have completely missed the point of everything you ever said to him, who didn't even fully understand the nature of this great task? Would you give it to someone who, on the face of it, had none of the necessary skills, and whose previous work experience bore little relation to what would now be required? Would you give it to someone whose personal life encompassed many responsibilities and distractions, including a sick mother-in-law?

Would you give it to someone young, with none of the saving grace of wisdom or experience, someone whose confident assertions of loyalty had a kind of youthful hubris about them? Would you give it to someone who was not even the person you felt closest to, not even the one you had the deepest affection for and had been known on occasion to lean upon? Would you entrust this precious task, for whose sake you had sacrificed everything, to someone whose only apparent claim to it lay in the fact that he loved you very greatly?

Of course you wouldn't. Not if you had any sense! It would be

the act of a fool! Which, by the standards of good business practice and common sense, is exactly what Jesus was. Because,
although he invited and attracted many followers, Peter was the
one he singled out to be the new leader, a rock on which to build.

In the times of the year when the media rediscover the
Christian story, in which Peter figures quite largely, I am always
intrigued to see that, whatever the treatment of this very dramatic
story, whether from a historical standpoint, from the perspective
of faith, or as modern interpretation, the picture we get of Peter
tends to vary very little. Almost invariably, he is portrayed as
older than the other disciples, as the steady, hardworking, pious
family man, a weighty, almost authoritarian figure among the
disciples. It seems clear that the *gravitas* that later came to be
attached to his successors has somehow been transferred to Peter
himself, the office describing the man, just as Judas is usually
portrayed as either tortured or cunning, Matthew as the archetypal sharp businessman, and John as beautiful and romantic. It
may of course be helpful in other contexts to think thus of Peter,
but when reflecting on the ministry to which Jesus called all his
followers, we need to remember the kind of man we meet in the
Gospels, who was the rock. He was proven unreliable, not only
unable to support Jesus publicly (and perhaps we might excuse
him that, for there was great danger in it), but unable even to stay
awake with him when it would have made a difference at no
cost to himself. Why Peter the liar? Why not, for example, the
disciple Nathaniel, of whom Jesus himself said 'There is nothing
false in this man'?

Peter's understanding was terribly limited; again and again, he
was the one who revealed his ignorance, who asked silly questions, who, even at the transfiguring moment on the mountaintop,
failed to comprehend the nature of what Jesus was doing. His
unsuitability to be the leader of a faith movement, a man who was
not learned in the law or in debating theology, whose language
was that of an uncouth Galilean, not the religious language of
priests and prophets, was apparent even to him. Like so many
before him, he too wanted to know 'Why me?' It is easy to
understand why after Jesus had called him to take care of his
sheep, he should turn to the man whom Jesus loved the most, to
John, and say 'But Lord, what about this man?'

And Peter was a young man, younger probably than Jesus –

'Young men, haven't you caught anything?' People married young, and died younger than we in the West do today. A young man, with a wife and a mother-in-law, and a boat, and perhaps even a family of little children – everything about him speaks of youth – his enthusiasm, his persistence in making a fool of himself, his extravagant love which crumbled the first time it was put to the test. Why Peter? What possible qualities did Jesus see in him to make him entrust the precious task to him?

We know that Jesus was the prophet of an upside-down-kingdom, one in which the values of the world were turned on their heads, where everything expected became everything unexpected, where the Messiah as military leader and victor was replaced by the Messiah as failure and sacrifice, where ends could become beginnings, and a new way of seeing God was demonstrated in making what had been thought of as untouchable – dirty feet, the sores of leprosy, the practitioners of the oldest profession, the bleeding of women – touchable and embraceable. We might choose to seek answers to the question, why Peter, in the possibility of as yet unexplored strengths. We might also, however, consider the possibility that it was in fact in his very failures, weaknesses and shortcomings, in his apparent utter unsuitability, that the answer to the question is to be found. Did Jesus choose Peter not in spite of his inadequacies but because of them?

Think for a minute of Peter fishing in Lake Tiberias, still unbearably vivid in his mind the events of the crucifixion, the crowing of the cock still ringing in his imagination. Think of what it is like to love someone very greatly, to protest that love at every opportunity, to want more than anything else an opportunity to prove your love. Then the moment comes – your love is called upon – and what do you do? – you make a mess of it, a complete and utter shambles, humiliatingly, bitterly, you fail, you fall apart. Remember the cross, the tomb, the despair – then the confusion, the conflicting reports, the hints of the unimaginable. What a turmoil for Peter, what alternating hope and fear, mixed with the question of how he could face this man, whom he had loved and then betrayed.

Then suddenly, at the water's edge, a man, talking to them, and then recognition. Not by Peter, as usual a little slow on the uptake, but by John, the disciple Jesus loved. It was John who saw – but it was Peter who acted, not waiting to ask John questions, not waiting for certainty, but out over the side and into the water, towards Jesus, moved only by love. And after they had eaten, Jesus talking to Peter. Not saying, as he had every right to say, 'Peter, you don't love me, you let me down', but saying, 'Peter, do you love me more than the others; then take care of my lambs.' Here was Jesus, giving him another opportunity to show his love; here was Jesus taking a chance on Peter. What would we not do for the people who go on taking a chance on us? What a human conversation, tinged as it was with all of Peter's sadness, and Jesus' too, but filled with hope and direction against all the odds. Peter's second-chance love has all the ache of lost innocence and idealism – he can tell that Jesus is struggling with trusting him, is asking again and again about his love – but it is stronger now, this love of Peter's. It is stronger with the power of real, forgiven love. '*Which one then, will love him more? It would be the one who was forgiven more.*'

And what about the inadequacy of Peter's understanding, his incessant foolish questions, his failure to comprehend. They had made him appear stupid – but they also made him a disciple, a seeker, a learner! And Jesus wanted his followers to be seekers, the teachers to be learners also, not people who had all the answers, who doled out enlightenment like commodity brokers, but people who were aware of their own need to seek truth, who would continue to question until the day they died. In Peter's blindness lay the seeds of his sight.

And what about the simple fisherman, unversed in religious language, untutored in the subtleties of theology. Fishing was in his blood; it was his vocation. In trouble, his instinct was not to pray or organize but to go fishing. But Jesus didn't seem to want a priest or a theologian. He wanted a fisherman. When Peter was first rushed to Jesus by his brother Andrew on the shores of Lake Galilee, he didn't know that he had taken a long road that would lead to Jerusalem and then to Rome. But it was the fisherman who was needed on that road when the priests and the theologians lost the way. It was the language of bread and fish and water and catches that spoke to the hearts of men and women, not the pieties of the religious. And it was the ordinary man, trauchled with the cares and responsibilities that are the lot of most of us, who took his wife and his life with him, who affirmed the life of faith as a possibility for all people burdened by life, not just as something for those set aside and apart. He had no refuge in religious formulae, no retreat into holier-than-thou posturing. Only his given self, following Jesus wherever that road led.

There are many forms of ministry, and we are all called to walk in different ways. But all of us are called as the people we are, not to some received picture of ministry. I find one of the most reassuring things about Peter is that he continued to be himself – impetuous, misguided, often getting it wrong. We read about him, for example, later on arguing with Paul and being severely dressed down for it. This endears him to me greatly, as someone who has many arguments with Paul. How comforting to know that Peter went on being himself, went on making mistakes, did not turn into some identikit model church leader. It is sometimes hard for us to make sense of how we experience God working in our lives; sometimes there seems to be so little rhyme or reason in what we're doing that it's tempting to try to make ourselves into what we think we ought to be, rather than discovering what we are. It is hard to believe that we are exactly the people needed, so inadequate do we feel. Well, Peter felt like that, and Moses and Samuel, and so even did Jesus in the Garden of Gethsemane. We are never alone in our fears. But, like Peter, perhaps we can learn that our love, however feeble, however flawed it seems, will be used, will matter, if we don't give up on it; and it will be that imperfect love, not the ideal love of our illusions, that will enable us to walk on the water.

Iona Abbey, April 1986.

25
Walking on Water

A Dialogue

Voice 1	Come!
Voice 2	I can't do it.
Voice 1	You can do it.
Voice 2	I'm too heavy. I'll sink.
Voice 1	Lay down your burdens and you'll be light enough.
Voice 2	I'm not strong enough.
Voice 1	You don't have to be strong. The water will hold you up.
Voice 2	I might get wet.
Voice 1	Yes, you will.
Voice 2	I might sink.
Voice 1	Only if you panic.
Voice 2	I might drown.
Voice 1	You won't drown. Just let yourself float, and the water will carry you.
Voice 2	People will see me.
Voice 1	Yes, they'll definitely see you. You might encourage some of them to try it too.
Voice 2	But some of them might try to stop me, for my own good.
Voice 1	Yes. But you can't live out of other people's fears.
Voice 2	Some of them might throw stones at me.
Voice 1	That's a risk you'll just have to take.
Voice 2	Some of them might laugh at me.
Voice 1	Yes. But you'll be the one walking on the water.
Voice 2	The water's very dark.

Voice 1   That's just because you're standing in the shadow. From here, it's a beautiful green.

Voice 2   There might be monsters.

Voice 1   Yes. But there are monsters where you are now.

Voice 2   How will I know which direction to walk in?

Voice 1   Just keep your eyes on me.

Voice 2   What if I can't see you for the waves?

Voice 1   I'll still be here.

Voice 2   I'm very scared.

Voice 1   We're all scared. But don't trust your fears. They're not reliable.

Voice 2   What will I trust?

Voice 1   Trust your love.

Voice 2   But what if I get that wrong?

Voice 1   Then trust my love. They come from the same place.

Voice 2   But what if . . . ?

Voice 1   This conversation's becoming very circular. I'm not going to stand here all day while you theorize. Now you have to move your body. Action will remove the doubt. Are you coming?

Iona Abbey, October 1992.

26
I've Seen You Before

A Maundy Thursday Conversation

Man   I've seen you before! You were there, weren't you, in the crowd? I noticed you, you weren't shouting like all the rest, but then afterwards I saw you picking up a branch from the road and you took it away somewhere. Why did you not shout?

Woman   You must be a very perceptive young man to have seen me. Most people never notice me. Most of the time I'm invisible. I like it that way. It gives me a lot of freedom. I come and go, I get into places you'd never believe. You see, I don't pose any threat to anyone.

    Why did I not shout? Well, I suppose it was because I've seen too many crowds in this city, shouting for too many heroes, hoping for too many saviours. They get on my nerves, these crowds, always wanting someone to take their risks for them.

Man   But didn't you think he was different? Don't you think we were shouting because we're fed up with the same old thing, the same old promises, the same tired old ways. That's what I want to think, anyway. I'm sick of cynics, and people who say, 'Oh well, it's always been this way and it always will, the rich get richer and the poor get shafted.' I want to come off the side-lines and get involved. I wanted to cheer, and it was a good feeling to be part of that crowd. Don't you think he's different?

Woman   Oh yes, I think he's different all right. It's not him I have the problem with. I just haven't seen any evidence that the crowd was different, that's all.

Man   But don't you think he can change us? He's obviously a man of God, that's clear. You know he's been performing miracles and healing people. Come on, you're a religious woman, I saw you in the temple, making your offering. You see, you're not as invisible as you think. Doesn't a religious woman like you think this man's going to be good for the people. Bring us back to God, back on the straight and narrow?

Woman   (*obviously offended*) I'll have you know that *in no way* am I a religious woman. I'm just somebody who slips into the temple now and again. I'm too poor and too busy to be religious. It takes a lot of effort to be religious – all that praying and sacrificing and keeping all these rules. And to tell you the truth, I don't set a lot of store by miracles. Not that it isn't very nice for the people they happen to, I'm sure, but I've seen such strange things in my life that a miracle here or there I tend to take for granted. No, I'm afraid it would take a lot more to impress me – something like this bunch of sheep who go baa every time a new sensation arrives in the city making a decision for themselves. Now *that* would be a miracle.

Man   I think the thing is, you haven't seen him close up. You haven't heard him talk, or sat beside him and seen how warm he is to people, even cripples and children. And he speaks with such power – oh, it's inspiring.

Woman   I can see you've got a bad case of hero-worship. Listen son, I told you before. It's not him I have the problem with. I've waited a lifetime for a leader to come along with the sense to know that beneath the trappings we're all the same – children, women, cripples and lepers, whores and Samaritans, swindlers and cheats, even the bloody Romans. We're all terrified and alone and messy and trying to beat down the things we think we should be ashamed of. Which aren't necessarily the

right things at all. It's just that some of us are better at
hiding it than others, that's all. But he knows that. He
can see through the mess to what's in the heart. He's at
home with the mess.

Man   But if you can see that about him, why don't you
accept him? Why don't you cheer, and follow him?
Are you afraid?

Woman   Did I say you were perceptive? I take it back. You're
remarkably foolish if you think it's all that simple. Of
course I accept him. That question is like saying, do
you accept your own life? But I *am* afraid. I'm afraid
for him. Not for me. What do I have to fear? I'm just
doing what I've always done. Do you know what I am?
I'm a servant. I have no one. My husband is dead, my
children are far away. So I wait on other people. I clear
up their messes, I cook their meals, I wash their dirty
feet. When they want me, I'm there. When they want
me to be invisible, which is most of the time, I disap-
pear. I'm the least important person in this city, the
lowest of the low. I don't matter to anyone. But if it
wasn't for me, this great city and all its important people would come crashing to the ground. No prayers
would be said, no children would be born, there would
be nothing to eat, there would be no temple, no law, no
teachers, nothing. People like me, we're like stones.
The city is built on us. Well, that's the way it's always
been, you might say. I know my place. But can't you
see what's happening? Don't you have eyes? They're
out to get this man, because he's like me!

Man   With all due respect to your grey hairs and your
advanced years, mother, I don't quite follow what you
mean. For a start, he's a man, and that puts him in quite
a different category. And he's learned in the Law; he
speaks words of wisdom, he performs great miracles.
And all the people are following him. I can't see any
way at all in which he's like you.

Woman   I was afraid of that. You idealistic young men, you
look for Messiahs to ride up and do heroic deeds – you

only honour knowledge and strength and the glamour of power. You want a leader, but he's a servant. He has no power.

Man   Of course he has power! Look how the people flock to him. I grant you he's not an obvious military leader, but there's more than one way to skin a cat.

Woman   He's not going to skin the cat. He's not going to lead a revolution – at least not the kind you mean. He's not here to throw out the Romans. He's a servant. He hasn't come to turn us all into priests and rulers. He's here to tell you that *I'm* the most important person in the city. He's here to tell you to be like me. I don't need to go rushing around after him. He and I, we know each other very well.

Man   (*outraged*) I think you're forgetting yourself, Madam. It's quite inconceivable that I should ever be like you. I am a man. And I have great tasks before me. I am wholly committed to the struggle to liberate my people.

Woman   (*wryly*) Quite so! And that is why I am afraid for him. He will be caught, trapped between the ones like you, unable to bear your disappointment when you finally get the message that the road leads through powerlessness, and the ones who are simply afraid of losing what power they have. And even more afraid of being exposed. Between you, you will grind him against the rock. You will betray him, through disappointment or through fear. You cannot stand servanthood, either of you. Come back and see me in a week, and tell me if I'm not right.

Man   You're talking nonsense, old woman. You will see that it will not be like that at all. (*curiously*) And what do *you* expect, anyway?

Woman   I expect to do what I have always done. I will wash the bodies of the dead, and I will prepare food for the mourners, and I will wait.

Man   What will you wait for?

Woman   I will wait for my time to come. I will wait and I will
         wait, and I will wait, for ever if need be, till people
         understand that I am the salt that flavours their earth,
         and the hunger that is not filled, and the bread that
         never runs out. And when one or two or a hundred
         believe that that is true, and when they give flesh to
         their belief, then your beaten hero will rise up out of
         his grave. But whenever they forget, and spit on the
         stones, and dress themselves in the garments of mas-
         tery, then they will push him back down, down into
         the tomb. And they will almost always forget. For you
         do not like servanthood. You think it demeans you.
         You will betray it.

Man   Crazy woman. We are not born for servitude, people
         like me. We are born for glory.

Woman   I did not say servitude. I am like him. I have made
         my choice. Well, we shall see which one of us is right,
         young man.

Man   What did you say your name was? . . .

Iona Abbey, 1990.

27
Liberation Day

Pentecost

You have shown me the paths that lead to life,
and your presence will fill me with joy.

(Acts 2.28)

Today, the day of Pentecost, we remember and celebrate with the Church throughout the world the coming of the Holy Spirit amongst the believers of the early Church. We remember the events of the day as we heard them described in the book of Acts, and we celebrate the fact that in the power of that Spirit of holiness, of wholeness, so many people have lived extraordinary lives, have shaped history in their living. It is a day for thanks, and in our prayer we will give thanks for people in whom we have seen and experienced the presence and the power of the Spirit.

But Pentecost is also a time for question and for reflection. Like every event of the Christian calendar, Pentecost only has real meaning if we allow it to challenge our own lives, to say to us, 'What does this mean for me, for my world, and not just for the world of the first century or the faith of other people?'

It is a mysterious story which is recounted in the Acts, full of images of wind and fire, of excitement and power. It is clear that here was an event which radiated power, energy, life. The crowd which gathered (and we need to remember that this quickly became a public event, not something shut away in a room, or even a church), were amazed by what was happening: confused, intrigued, and many openly sceptical, accusing the believers of drunkenness.

It is, perhaps, more difficult for us to reconstruct the Pentecost event in our imagination than the Christmas or the Easter story, which are more familiar both in our religious teaching and in our art. We have more images to call on, more pictures to help us with our rehearsal of the drama. We may even find the mysteriousness of Pentecost, our inability to make it concrete, frightening. Power is always awesome, especially when it seems to have broken out of the realm of our everyday experience. This story of fervent disciples, large, polyglot crowds, noise, confusion, rushing winds and tongues of fire is too elemental, too raw for us to feel quite comfortable with it. Well, that's all right. The power of God is not something we should ever feel too comfortable about. But our fear should not prevent us from allowing the Pentecost experience to touch us. Let's leave what was actually happening that day for a little and think about the effect that it had on the believers.

Its first consequence was that all the barriers of language were broken down. Somehow, people communicated with each other, no matter what their native tongue, in a manner that meant that everyone could understand. And they were able to talk to the crowd in the same fashion. Strangers, foreigners, outsiders, a crowd of as many different races and nations as Jerusalem, that crossroads city, could gather, heard these Galileans talk to them in their own languages. In the power of the Spirit, the believers broke out of the prison of race, and were able to announce good news and be heard. And such was the conviction with which they spoke, so evident their commitment, that many people trusted their good news and were baptized.

The second consequence of Pentecost for the believers was evident in their life together. We read in the Acts that all the believers continued together in close fellowship and shared their belongings with one another, selling their property and possessions and distributing the money amongst all, according to what each one needed. They met together, they shared meals and they were joyful. Every day, more people joined them. In the power of the Spirit, the believers broke through the barriers of class and property and possessions, and created a common life, a life of justice and care for those in need. Jew and Gentile, slave and free, male and female, all the age-old barriers of Jewish society were shattered, as people were gathered up into this new body, and embraced gladly.

And a third consequence of the Pentecost experience for the believers was that suddenly they were filled with a new power. Suddenly, they found the confidence to do things they had never dreamed of; suddenly, ordinary people found that they could move mountains. Miracles and wonders is how the Acts describes it, miracles of sharing and healing and transformation, wonders of love and courage and endurance done by people empowered by the Spirit.

It is a never-ending story, because Pentecost happens whenever people begin to live empowered by the Spirit of Jesus. It is a Spirit which gives gifts to those who live in it, a Spirit which bears fruit in their lives, and these gifts and these fruits are described many times in the New Testament. But I want just now to return to the first Pentecost, and to ask with the crowd, 'What does this mean?' We know the consequences for the believers of the coming of the Spirit, and we have seen its presence in history, in the church, and in people we know. But we need to know what happened to people that it had this effect on them. We know the outward facts, but we want to understand and to share the inward reality. If Pentecost is not rooted in our own experience, then it is a flame that will soon die. We may speak in tongues, we may wish to live guided by the Spirit, we may seek community, but if the Spirit of the living God has not burned a path down into the depth of our experience, then Pentecost still awaits us.

If Christmas is the festival of the incarnation, and Easter is the festival of the resurrection, then Pentecost is the festival of the liberation. Because what Pentecost is about is freedom. It is about the Holy Spirit setting people free. Of course, that freedom was already theirs, demonstrated by the life and death and resurrection of Jesus, but Pentecost is when they realized their freedom, and when it entered their experience. All the barriers by which people are bound and divided had been cut away, and suddenly they saw the truth – they were not bound by their own past of guilt and fear, they were not bound by a weight of failure they could never hope to compensate for. They were free. It is almost as if the forgiveness and the new life they had believed in since the empty tomb had needed till now to strike them. We also know that experience. How many of us have received good news, which we repeat over and over to ourselves, and yet somehow it doesn't seem real, until, much later perhaps, the joy of it suddenly sweeps over us with the greatest intensity, glee even. From being believers, people who believed in their freedom, they became knowers, people who experienced the freedom of that forgiveness. No wonder things got out of hand. No wonder people thought they were drunk. I've seen pictures of VE Day, of Paris being liberated and of London going wild after peace was declared. The sense of release communicated is almost unbearable! Well, Pentecost is liberation day for Christians. That's what Peter must have been realizing when he spoke so passionately to the crowd: 'God raised him from death, setting him free from its power, because it was *impossible* that death should hold him prisoner.' And as for Jesus, so for us the words ring true: 'You have shown me the paths that lead to life, and your presence will fill me with joy.'

The freedom I'm talking about is not, I think, freedom from responsibility or from care or from suffering. It would be naïve in the extreme to think that. If anything, it is freedom *for* all these things in greater measure. It is not freedom to be relieved of the necessity of making decisions and wanting to 'let the Spirit lead me'. This can often be simply a dissociation from assuming responsibility for *our* actions, and is a kind of handing over of freedom. Nor is it freedom to indulge in cosy, happy 'togetherness', shutting out our own or others' pain. Such is the kind of dangerous illusion that we all fall prey to from time to time. It is freedom from bondage, freedom from enslavement to idols – the idols of wealth, status, success, race, family, the idol of our past or our bad image of ourselves, the idol of politics or religion or the Bible or the church. These bonds were broken at Pentecost, and people became free-spirited, not chained to things they had done in the past, not chained to things people had done to them. Whatever happened, whatever human prison they found themselves in, they could respond with a new freedom, as free people have done in camps and gaols and gulags in our own century.

We may not experience the liberation of Pentecost in the same way as the disciples. For us, it may be slower, quieter, more like the flowing water than the rushing wind or the tongues of fire. There will be many times when we forget that we are free, and return to the old habits of our captivity, as the Israelites did in the desert. I expect it took people many days and weeks to get used to lighted windows after the black-out of the war. But Jesus defeated the power of death, and so may we wherever it looms. This is the promise, and Pentecost happens when we experience the truth of the promise. We can change, we can be free, and the Spirit of life not death is powerful in and for us, when we realize that we *are* loved, whatever and whoever we are and have been. But the Spirit of life cannot be contained or possessed or locked up, and it moves also in the lives of those from whom we are divided or alienated – enemies, opponents, those we have hurt or done injustice to, those who have hurt or done injustice to us. The Spirit is indivisible, and will sweep us into a recognition of our connection with others, and this we must engage with if we do not want to re-erect the barriers within ourselves. We cannot live empowered by the Spirit if there are rocks of hate or pride blocking its free movement. So we also have some work to do, to keep ourselves open to the Spirit, the hard and painful work of freedom. But there is no more creative and ecstatic work!

We still need Pentecost in our lives, and in the life of the world. Everywhere people are groaning in bondage to the idols of racism and greed, of war and oppression. Everywhere, people are crying out for release from the prisons of fear and bitterness. And yet, today, all across the world, people will also demonstrate their freedom in the fruits of love, joy, peace, patience, goodness, kindness, faithfulness, humility, self-discipline. This is their liberation day. We pray that it will also be a liberation day for us.

Iona Abbey, 1986.

28
On the Border

Michaelmas

When I was a child visiting Iona, I was always fascinated by a rather ugly piece of art in one of the chapels round the Abbey. It was a wood carving of a disembodied hand holding up a great sword, and I remember finding it curious, disquieting, and strangely threatening. It did not fit in, either with my maps of the world, nor with my maps of faith, greatly shaped as they were by the flowing Celtic imagery and the flowing Western seas of Iona. Later I learned that the sword was a symbol of the archangel Michael, whose chapel it was, and whose feast, along with all the angels, falls tomorrow in the church's calendar.

But, being a Presbyterian, my disquiet, my fear and fascination, were never really addressed. Apart from a rush of wings in a starry sky over Bethlehem, and an equally brief appearance in a garden tomb, angels are mostly severely ignored in Presbyterian preaching, along with many other somewhat chaotic and uncontrollable things we prefer not to think about. But inexorably, over the years since my first encounter with Michael and his flaming sword, angels have been catching up with me. Finally, I have come to the point of turning and facing them full on. And I have to say that it has been their evocation in literature and cinema that has intrigued me far more than anything in theology or the church: Rainer Maria Rilke, the great German poet, giving up therapy, because 'if I lose my demons, I will lose my angels too'; Wim Wenders, in *Wings of Desire*, with Bruno Ganz coming as an angel to earth in a circus, and falling in love with a woman.

But mostly because I have become more and more aware that,

at times in my life, I have had experiences for which the most appropriate description has corresponded to the words of George MacLeod's great prayer, which begins, 'Give us a message . . . send us an angel that will start us seeking a new way of life.' Sometimes, though it may seem uncomfortably irrational, I have had the feeling of having entertained angels unawares.

But what do I find, when I turn to confront the angels? If I were a cynic, I might respond that angels have a habit of showing up when human beings want someone else to assume responsibility for what we secretly want to do anyway. 'It was an angel', 'an angel said it would happen this way' – whether that should be the invasion and conquest of someone else's country (oh, the poor Canaanites) the destruction of one's internal enemies (remember the 70,000 Israelites slaughtered by the angel of the Lord in the time of David) or the explanation of highly irregular sexual encounters (Lot's virgin daughters offered up to save the angels) or even pregnancies. But I'm not a cynic.

If I were an anthropologist, angels would teach me a great deal about the world-view of the early Hebrews, with their strong belief that the human personality is open to invasion by the Spirit of God, so that sometimes actors in a story were described as men and sometimes as angels. And about the fact that our strict division between the natural and the supernatural was much less strict, much more blurred, for them, taken for granted, in fact. And I would remark the fact that in the time of the later Old Testament writing, the distance between the human and the divine had become great enough to require the presence of intermediaries, of go-betweens, bridging the gap between heaven and earth. The immanent God, God moving among people, had become the transcendent God, distant, out of reach. But I'm not an anthropologist.

And if I were a sociologist, I might take pleasure in the fact that so communitarian were the people of Israel in outlook and way of life, so far from the later individualism that has marked much of recent Western culture, that the notion of a lonely, isolated divine being was inconceivable. God required a community, a court of heaven, servants and companions. God needed angels, in order not to be alone. And the early Christian world-view, where conviction of God's presence with the body of Christ found expression in the profound belief in ministering spirits, guardian angels, to individuals and churches alike. But I'm not a sociologist.

And if I were a psychologist, I could really go to town on angels. I could see them as archetypal patterns for people and species. I could regard them as manifesting the spirituality, the interiority of times and places and people. I could project all qualities and characteristics of good on to them, as I could all evil on to demons. And as a moral philosopher, I could see them as symbolic of the eternal cosmic battle between good and evil. But I am neither a psychologist nor a moral philosopher.

I am a person of faith, for whom the crucial questions are not in the end theoretical but practical. Not 'what does this mean', but 'what does this mean for me? How, therefore, must I act?' Where does this point me on the journey of my life, which is inevitably the journey guided by my convictions?

I am informed and challenged and enlarged in my faith journey by the discoveries of biblical scholars and anthropologists, of artists and sociologists, of psychologists and philosophers, yes, and even of cynics. Goodness knows that there is enough evidence in the inexhaustible library of Scripture and tradition to support many of their findings. But I also know that for me, map-making is no substitute for walking the road. As I take a pause on that road, a citizen of the planet earth approaching a millennium, is the notion of angels simply an irrelevant anachronism, enculturated in other histories, other geographies? Or is there some deeper significance in them which can transcend forms, be transformed into something that is true to my experience? And I remember that the hand of Michael, grasping its sword, filled me with strange unease, with fear and fascination, before I had ever read any biblical criticism, or sociology or psychology.

In 1979, I gave birth to my first son, David. In 1981, my second son, Duncan, was born. My sons were planned, prepared for, properly organized to arrive at a mutually convenient time. They were a life choice – they felt like the work of their father and me. In 1983, without planning or premeditation, our daughter Helen was born. She came kicking and screaming into life at the worst possible time – we had both just started new jobs, moved far from our families, and into a house which was being renovated around us. She came like a kick in the pants from God to remind us that actually we didn't have life all tied up and neatly labelled.

She came to remind us that before ever we chose life, life had chosen us.

I tell that story because it reminds me of birth. And birth reminds me of angels. Birth is a profound moment, a profound process, whether it be the birth of a child, or of a work of art, the birth of a new idea or insight, or the birth of a new part of us. Or indeed, a new birth of us, a conversion, a being born again.

It is a moment of power. It is a moment of struggle. It is a moment of transformation. It is a moment when we stand on the border between the human and the divine. And what I observe, in Scripture, and in the experience of the church, is that these moments come accompanied by angels. Let me try to unpack that a little.

First of all, moments of power. I do not stand here as a self-created being, the work of my own hands. My life is already given. I am a tiny, and yet quite dynamic force. We are so accustomed, or perhaps I should say addicted, in our society, to the notion of being in control, so removed, most of us, from the elemental struggles of survival, that we have few opportunities of allowing ourselves to enter, even a little, into the awesomeness, the uncontrollable mystery, of the power of life, that also expresses itself uniquely in the wild violet and the cockroach and the raging sea. I remember being in labour with one of my children, and as a particularly acute wave of pain washed over me, trying to get down off the bed and saying to those around me somewhat hysterically – 'I think it's time to stop now. I'm just going to go home.' And being rather offended as they all fell about laughing. The small but determined life inside me was not in the least interested in my pain or my feelings, just that I should do what I had been chosen to do – co-operate with the mighty surge into life it was making. A moment of power. And in the Scriptures, and in tradition, moments of power – the power of birth, of sexuality, of love, of creativity, of aggression or self-assertion or destruction, in human beings and in nature – come accompanied by angels. It is annunciation. They are messengers of power that is outwith our control.

And for me, it is important to remark these annunciations, to look for the angels that draw my attention to moments of power. Because we do not understand the awesome power of life, and because in our so-called enlightened culture, we are afraid of everything we cannot label and possess and tie down, we become afraid of life. And because we are afraid, we try to tame and restrict and sanitize and legislate and reduce life. And what we can't control we ultimately, too often, seek to destroy. I need angels to remind me that there is a huge difference between the fear of God that is awe in the face of mystery, and the wretched cowardice that would destroy what it cannot control. The first worships, and finds grace and courage to live. The second denies, and finds death by degrees.

And moments of struggle. In my experience, the greatest struggles in life are not between black and white, between the good and the bad. Life is not simplistic in that way. We wrestle much more with shades of grey, between one almost good and another, with trying to discern what is good and what is best. Always in the knowledge that even what we do with the best intentions may have the worst results . . . the good that we would we do not . . . is not a moral statement, it is an ontological one. Abraham on the mountain with Isaac, Jacob wrestling a blessing at Bethel, Jesus in the wilderness, being offered such socially responsible options by Satan, and, especially, Jesus in Gethsemane. And all of these accompanied by angels. When we go into the wilderness, the real danger is not in the struggle. The real danger is in refusing the struggle. Perhaps that's what Rilke meant, when he said that he feared that if his demons were taken away from him, his angels would depart too. I have come to value my demons. Without them, I would never have encountered my guardian and ministering angels. Without the struggle of labour, there is no new creation.

And moments of transformation. In giving birth, we are always changed, whether physically or spiritually. We are not the same as before, we have taken on new forms that are the other side of labour. We have gone across. All the sacraments of the church recognize this deep truth. They hold up for us the means of transformation. The second birth of baptism that is the transformation of our first birth requires us to go through the waters of repentance, of turning in a new direction. The breaking of bread that is the transformation of the brokenness of life which otherwise leads only to death. Broken, not to be stuck together, but to be shared out, to make the broken places sing. Womb and tomb, incarnation and crucifixion, both crying out for resurrection, for the transformation of life and death, both come accompanied by angels. Look out for angels around moments of birth and death. I'm sure you'll see them when you look.

And finally, moments when we stand on the border between the human and the divine. When we experience the power that is greater than us, when we struggle or wrestle or labour, embrace the desert. when we participate in the transformation of our creativity into new forms, we are always where we have been taken to the limits of our experience, to the extremity of life. For a moment, we have broken through the weary repetitiveness of unredeemed life into the life of the kingdom, into the new creation, into the life eternal. By the grace of God, that life is always there, waiting to break through, in the words of George MacLeod, 'The air of the eternal seeping through the physical, the everlasting glory dipping into time, where turn but a stone and an angel moves'. By the love of Jesus Christ, we are offered a way of birth and struggle and transformation through which to live in freedom with the awesome power of the Holy Spirit. And so we come to the border, and the promise of Jesus to Nathaniel is of an ultimate border crossing into the new creation. And angels patrol the border. Or, in the beautiful imagery of Old and New Testaments, they come and go on the stairway to heaven. So I have begun to look for angels at times when I have a faint sight of the border, an intimation of the eternal seeping through the physical. And, since I have experienced these always as very painful and difficult times, and find the glory only in the deepest grey, I know now why I shivered at the sight of the hand of Michael with the piercing sword upraised. But I believe I have also encountered angels.

> '. . . send us an angel that will start us seeking a new way of life . . .'

> (George MacLeod)

Birth and death come accompanied by angels.
And sometimes, maybe always,
the moment of encounter is the same.

Annunciation – 'you will be changed,
you will give birth to something new.'
And the guardians of the tomb –

'He is not here.
Why do you seek the living
among the dead?'

Lot or Lot's wife-like,
poised between the no-longer and the not-yet,
this I can understand.
This I can, albeit painfully,
give my assent to.

But why did no one warn me
how terrifying angels are?

They are not nice and reassuring,
all dressed in white.
They come with flashing eyes,
and carry flaming swords to pierce your heart.
They come with ruthlessness.

Still, they teach you one thing,
these messengers of God.

I have learned the proper fear of the Lord.

And with this fear, I wait for death, and birth.

Now glory be to the Father and to the Son and to the Holy Spirit,
as it was in the beginning, is now and ever shall be, world without end. Amen.

*Northern Federation for Training in Ministry, Eucharist,
28 September 1993.*

29
The Tears of the Sower and the Songs of the Reaper

Harvest Thanksgiving

James 4.13–18; Mark 4.26–32

Our ancestors, the ones who are so far back in time that their names are not recorded, feared the darkness. It represented for them all that was unknown, hard to understand, wild, mysterious and threatening. And so they loved the sun, and welcomed its coming each day, and the coming of the long days of summer. Their lives were hard, working the earth and the sea in order to win their daily bread, a constant encounter with nature, carrying out in sweat and tears the necessary tasks of living – digging the soil, planting the seed, building a shelter, cherishing the fire, giving birth and burying, and always waiting and praying. And as well, always the attempt to understand, to give meaning to their lives, to make sense of their suffering and joy. So they told stories, painted pictures and sang songs, and made ceremonies of the sun that held truth as they understood it, and feasted to celebrate the triumph of life against all the odds.

And of all their ceremonies, perhaps the most important was the harvest celebration. The long days were coming to an end, the sun was going down, and winter was approaching. This was a crucial time, when they would discover if their toil during the spring and summer had been enough to keep them in bread throughout the long, dark days of winter, when nothing grows. It was the time when they would discover if their efforts had been granted nature's blessing of an abundant harvest. So their harvest celebration was quite literally one of the triumph of life over

126

death, for if the harvest was bad there would be empty bellies and full coffins.

Jesus too was familiar with the struggle for life, with the unchanging cycle of the seasons and the planting and harvesting, with the corn and the wine, the fish and the well. His stories and parables are full of these images, for he knew they were the things of life for his people. And though his time seems to us less harsh, less precarious, than that of our prehistoric ancestors, the demands of the necessary tasks of life were still there in every story he told, in every home he visited, in every life he touched. The struggle to understand, to find meaning, still remained, by now written in law and announced by prophets. And Jesus' time and people too had their ceremonies: the dedication of a child, a wedding, the anointing for burial – and among them, the celebration of the harvest.

We are far from that world. It has a strangeness and yet an attraction for us, who receive our bread ready sliced and wrapped in plastic, our (mostly) clean water at the turn of a tap, our heat and light at the touch of a switch, and our recreation from the technology of our time. *Our* feasts are indulgent, and our ceremonies of life, divorced from any notion of us as creatures, have become cynical and second-rate.

The past seems odd and unsophisticated, the stuff of movies and furnishing fabrics. And yet it is we who are the odd ones out. For the vast majority of people in this world, and for some living in the midst of this society, the demands of life are still urgent and immediate – for bread (never mind the jam), for clean water, for shelter and heat and light. And harvest celebrations are still for them real and powerful and immediate because they mean the difference between life and death in a way they don't for us – life or death in famine-ridden Somalia, life or death in drought-stricken Zimbabwe. For most people in the world, a feast is still a special occasion which is a celebration of sufficiency, not excess. For the human spirit, there is all the difference in the world between the feast that is an expression of the boredom of too much, and the feast that is the expression of the delight of enough.

It is quite easy for celebration of fruitfulness in the cities of the Western world to become empty and meaningless, to become simply an over-spiritualized, casual kind of thanks for things we take for granted because the nearest we get to their production is when we pick them off the supermarket shelves. It would be easy for us to forget that just like the poorest peasant, we are utterly dependent on the cycle of the seasons and the abundance of the harvest, simply because our society has greater purchasing power than Bangladesh, or a more temperate climate than Malawi. It can be easy for us to reduce God to a kind of fairy godmother out there, who comes around to give us a spiritual lift when we are feeling low, just because we are so accustomed now to thinking that we are in control, that we can do anything, that we are the creator not the creature. But for us to act thus would be to deny reality. Reality is that we need to celebrate fruitfulness just as much as our ancestors, because even in cities far removed from the land, we are as dependent as the peasant farmer or crofter on the promise of the harvest. Reality is that we confident and prosperous nations (and, even in the present economic crisis, we are still prosperous) who protect ourselves from the effects of bad harvest, surpluses and shortages, are in fact far more damaging and dangerous to the earth than the poor of the countries of the South, that our overconsumption, pollution, wastefulness and market-driven economies are threatening the very earth itself. Reality is that we are created to be interdependent, not just with other human beings, but with the earth. This magnificent, fragile and precious planet which is all our home, needs us to live in right relationship with it, and each of us with each other, if we are not all to perish. Jesus embodied what it means to live in right relationship – gently, generously, justly and lovingly – with the earth, with each other.

We cannot un-become what we are. For most of us visiting Iona are not farmers or peasants, fisherfolk or countryfolk, though we may have our roots among these. We are city people – we walk on concrete among busy traffic in crowded streets. Many of us don't even have gardens in which to observe the changing of the seasons. The signs of the harvest, the rich colours of autumn may not have the same meaning for us as they do for country people. But they may have an equally profound meaning. They may help us to remember that we need to live in greater harmony with the earth, and take ever more seriously the efforts being made in our society to help us be responsible earth-dwellers. They may remind us that the task of proclaiming God's kingdom requires not just generosity in giving, but a greater measure of justice. We might take a little time to give thanks for a great harvest sown and reaped by our ancestors – of children raised, of faithful working lives, of care for neighbours, of service to the community, of wisdom shared. And we might think of what kinds of seeds we are sowing in our communities, in our cities, in our country. Are they seeds that will bring forth young people who believe they are valued, encouraged and supported as they struggle to grow? Are they seeds of friendship that will bring forth a harvest of neighbourliness and mutual respect in this multi-cultural society? Are they seeds of justice and love that will bring forth a harvest of caring and sharing in a world of hurt and division? Are they seeds of reverence and cherishing of the earth and all living things that will bring forth healing and renewal?

The letter of James which we heard read, says 'Goodness is the harvest that is produced from the seeds the peacemakers plant in peace.' We can plant seeds for good harvest. We had better, for as we sow, so shall we reap. It doesn't matter if they are only tiny seeds, and seem insignificant. We cannot usually know the effect of what we plant; nor are we required to worry about success, only about faithfulness; nor take responsibility for ends, only for means. The gospel reminds us that it is the mustard seed, the smallest of all seeds, which grows up to become the biggest of all the plants – and the birds come and make their nests in its shade.

We don't make the harvest happen. Like the sower of seed in Jesus' story, the seeds sprout and grow, and we do not know how it happens. It is still God who gives the harvest, God's spirit that works in ways we do not understand. It is our part in the labour of creation to plant the kind of seeds that will bring about a good harvest, and then, when they have grown, to bring them in so that they do not stand rotting and redundant in the fields. These small seeds of love are as vital to our survival as the seeds planted by peasants and farmers; that harvest of people and their gifts is as necessary to the human spirit as the corn and fruit to see us through the winter.

> Over and over, yes, deeper and deeper, my heart is pierced through with earth's sorrowing cry.
> But the tears of the sower and the songs of the reaper shall mingle together in joy by and by.

In the name of the Creator and of the Son and of the Holy Spirit. Amen.

Iona Abbey, 4 October 1992.

30
Unravelling the Gordian Knot

Remembrance Day

What the Lord requires of us is this; to do what is just,
to show constant love, and to live in
humble fellowship with our God.

(Micah 6.8, GNB)

Remembrance Day seems an appropriate time to think in the light of our Christian faith about our actions as individuals and as citizens of our country, especially as we seem to be moving ever closer to the outbreak of war in the Gulf. Historically, Christians have adopted a wide range of attitudes towards war, from the extreme belligerence of the Crusaders, who thought they had the right to impose by force their own beliefs on people of another faith, and to occupy, annex and ravage their lands in the process, to the pacifism of the Society of Friends, the Quakers, for whom it is an article of faith that they will not take another life. And, indeed, it is possible to select individual texts from the Bible to justify almost any position; it is not only possible, but widely practised.

But I do not intend to join that exercise, or to claim that I have the answers to the problems of war. Rather, I want to take a broader look at the context in which we, as Christians, live our lives. I want to talk about means and ends.

In the Shorter Catechism, which all Presbyterians used to learn and be tested on, the first question was: 'What is man's chief end?' And the answer was: 'Man's chief end is to glorify God'. And of course it goes without saying that glorifying God is not simply the words that we use in worship and prayer, it is also the actions whereby we practise what we preach. To worship God means to give God worth. We glorify God by giving the best of what we have and what we are. And this glory is, for Christians, the meaning of our lives, our *raison d'être*, our primary responsibility – and when we do it wholeheartedly, it is our delight as much as our duty. It is a wonderful and awesome thing, it is an enormous *yes* to the life we have, a yes to the whole creation.

For it is also unquestionable what God's end for humankind is.

I have come that you might have life, life in all its fullness.

Do not be afraid, little flock. It is your Father's pleasure to give you the kingdom.

For God so loved the world that he sent his only son, that whoever believes in him may not die, but have eternal life.

The whole thrust of the dynamic power of God is towards our good, our well-being. It is an end of love.

And where God's end for us and our end as human beings meet and coincide, the result is a magnificent harmony. It is like a love affair where the attraction does not fade, the bloom is not worn away, the communication does not cease. It is like a wedding day, a mutual delight. It is a covenantal relationship. And indeed, it seems as if God is irrevocably attracted to us. And yet despite the blessings of this earth, despite the potential that life has to offer us, being human we betray the relationship. We do not give the best of our lives. We are spoilers, and most of all we are spoilers of the image of God reflected in the faces of other human beings.

And yet God cannot resist loving us, and has sought ways to invite us back into relationship. Prophets have always been one way. But when people did not hear their passionate declaration of the love of God, God did not abandon us. Christians speak of Jesus as the way. If God's end is that we have life in all its fullness, life in right relationship with all that is, including the depths of the mystery of God, Jesus is the gate through which we pass, his way our way, the means to our end.

God's end and God's way. But what about *our* way? This way must mean for us something more than just a clichéd attachment to a meaningless statement, a pious platitude devoid of content.

If Jesus is the way in which God comes close to us, then he is also a two-way street. We follow him towards God, towards the life in which we are not divided from the ultimacy of our lives. If we look to the prophets whose prophecies Jesus continually pointed to, we find people asking the same questions – how do we glorify God, they asked. Is it by offering sacrifices, by giving huge amounts of our wealth, by praying loudly, is it even by offering our sons to be killed? *How*? is always the crucial question. 'No, it is not these ways', says the prophet Micah. 'The Lord has told us what is good. What he requires of us is this . . . to do what is just, to show constant love, to walk in humble fellowship with our God.' What God requires of us are still these same things. These are the way of Jesus, whom we follow and who followed them through death. They are our way – the way to fullness of life.

Having said that, I want to suggest that our discipleship demands of us that we should be greatly concerned with ways and unconcerned about ends. If we accept this picture of God's desire for us as our chief end, not just as a nice theory but into the practice of our lives, then from there we concentrate on the way to realize it. This is another way of saying that we do not put our trust in our own plans and powers and agendas.

It is not our task to save the world, or the church, or the nation. It is not our task to tell other people how to live their lives, or to design master schemes for saving them from themselves. God has given people free will to make choices about their lives, and it is not up to us to decide for them. Because if we do, we are taking on the role of playing God in their lives. To have ends in the world we live in is to seek to control, to manipulate, to impose and to dominate. That is absolutely not to suggest that we are not involved in the world, in the church, in the nation or in the community. It is rather to suggest that in all of these our task is to do what is just, to show constant love, and to walk in humble fellowship with God. The only life we have the right to control is our own. We are personally responsible. But we are personally responsible within a whole network of relationships. So we must struggle to discern what it means to do what is just towards our families, our friends, our colleagues, our fellow-citizens, and all our fellow-human beings. And we must struggle to do what is just out of an attitude of constant love in all of these relationships, a love that recognizes that we are fallible and fragile and make mistakes and need forgiveness and are precious. And living in right relationship will incline us towards the realization that in the eyes of God we are no more important than the least important in the world's eyes – but no less important either. Walking humbly with God will help us to see and treat others in a less cavalier fashion. When we are humbled by the love and tenderness of another for us, we become more tender and loving towards others.

If we are not faithful and obedient in our ways, then it does not matter how exalted our ends are. If we pursue good ends by bad means, then the ends themselves will be corrupted. This is one of my grave concerns in the present crisis in the Gulf. I accept that the end of wishing to deter aggression and the violation of sovereign territory is a legitimate one. But I have not been able to see either that this is a principle that has been constantly applied, or that the ways that have brought us to this point have been good. To be presented now with a protestation of just ends is cynical in the extreme. Did we, nations of the West, not care about just ends when we were supplying vast quantities of arms to Saddam Hussein when Iraq was pursuing an aggressive war against Iran, nor when Palestine or the Lebanon was having its sovereign territory invaded, nor when the people of East Timor were suffering genocide at the hands of Indonesia? We are reaping a whirlwind of our own making. Western ends in the Gulf and the Middle East over this century have continually used the same means we now condemn. We have not done what is just, we have not shown constant love, we have not walked humbly with our God.

And now, I have a great fear that the declaration of war will prove to be a much greater ill than the one we seek to redress. In such a war there will be great military casualties. There could be ecological devastation whose effects will be felt for hundreds of years. And, such is the nature of modern warfare, there will be huge loss of civilian life – old people and children, as well as other civilian men and women. In the First World War, military casualties outnumbered civilian ones by a huge number. In the Second World War, there were two civilian deaths for every military one. In Vietnam, the ratio was 20 civilian deaths for every military death. Biological warfare, chemical warfare, all the paraphernalia of modern warfare kill indiscriminately. I am not convinced that there is no other way, that we have exhausted every other means of resolving this conflict. Until I am convinced of that, I cannot follow the voice which calls for war. I do not recognize that voice as the voice which calls me.

That conclusion is my personal responsibility. I do not seek to impose it on anyone else. And in order for my conclusion to have integrity, I have to be able to demonstrate that if I apply criteria of justice, love and humility towards the actions of others, then I must apply them with even greater rigour towards my own actions. I must continually and prayerfully strive to do what is just, to show constant love and to walk humbly with God in all that I do. I understand that there are many who would consider this to be a naïve and foolish stance. I know that it does not answer every question, nor do I think it is possible to have simple answers – there is no cutting of the Gordian knot, which must rather be 'patiently unravelled', in the words of Robert Louis Stevenson. I know that it is terribly painful to resist the temptation to bring about speedy ends, out of our longing for resolution, and I know that the suffering that is and will be most involved in this conflict will not be mine. But we so easily forget the true horrors of war. We cannot be other than compromised. Nevertheless, within that taint that we all bear, we each have to decide where we stand. You are free to draw your own conclusions about the present situation. That is your God-given right. But it is your God-given responsibility to consider seriously and prayerfully to what extent the events in the Gulf are consistent with the way of Christ, and with the end of glorifying God.

Lansdowne Church, Glasgow, 1990.